YOUR LEADERSHIP LEGACY

Becoming the Leader You Were Meant to Be

LTC(R) Oakland McCulloch

Oakland McCulloch

Skrive Publications
Miramar Beach, FL
U.S.A.

Printed in the U.S.A.

Cover design by Liz Nitardy

ISBN 978-1-952037-12-2 (hardcover)
ISBN 978-1-952037-10-8 (paperback)
ISBN 978-1-952037-25-2 (eBook)
LCCN 2021901077

*Skrive*publications
Copy Editing • Proofreading • Publishing

www.skrivepublications.com

Dedication

I dedicate this book to my family who allowed me to go on this great journey as a leader in the Army. It was not always easy on them, but they always supported me. I especially need to thank my loving wife for her support throughout the years. She really is my best friend, my biggest fan, my biggest supporter and my biggest critic. Without her, I doubt I would be where I am today and none of this would have been possible.

I also dedicate this book to the outstanding leaders, soldiers and others with whom I've had the privilege of working. They allowed me to learn how to be a leader, and they allowed me to make mistakes along the way. For that I will be forever grateful.

Table of Contents

Foreword

I met Oakland McCulloch in January, 1985, when he joined
the Huskie Army ROTC Battalion at Northern Illinois
University as a transfer student. From the beginning, it was
apparent he had something the rest of us did not have. We
were all struggling to learn how to write an Operations Order
(OPORD) for battle. As a brand new student, Oak organized a
study group in order to show us how to do it. Our whole class
showed up! He has continued to display a lifetime of selfless
service and a desire for excellence in all endeavors. He is a true
leader in every sense of the word, and more importantly, a
leader of leaders.

-Kelly Anne (Smyth) McCulloch, Napoleon's Corporal

About the Author

Oakland McCulloch was born in Loudon, Tennessee, and raised in Kirkland, Illinois. After graduating from Hiawatha High School, he attended the United States Military Academy at West Point for two years. He then graduated from Northern Illinois University and received his commission as an infantry officer through the Reserve Officer Training Corps in 1986.

During his 23-year career in the Army, Oak McCulloch held numerous leadership positions in the Infantry and Armor branches. He assisted in disaster relief operations for Hurricane Hugo in Charleston, South Carolina, and Hurricane Andrew in South Florida. His operational deployments included Operation Desert Shield/Desert Storm in Saudi Arabia and Iraq where he served as a general's aide-de-camp. He was also the Congressional Liaison Officer in support of operations in Bosnia and the operations officer during a peacekeeping deployment to Kosovo. He held instructor positions at the U.S. Army Ordnance School, the U.S. Army Command and General Staff College, the Australian Command and Staff College, the University of South Alabama and Stetson University. His last position in the Army was a three-year tour as Professor of Military Science at the University of South Alabama where he led the training and commissioning of lieutenants and tripled the size of the program during his tenure.

LTC McCulloch retired from the Army in September, 2009, with over 23 years of active service and joined the staff at the Bay Area Food Bank in Mobile, AL, as the associate director. He was also the Vice Chair for Military Affairs on the Mobile Area Chamber of Commerce and a member of the Mobile Rotary International Club. LTC McCulloch left the food bank in December, 2010, to become the Senior Military Science Instructor and recruiter for the Army ROTC program at Stetson University in DeLand, Florida. During his nine years at Stetson, the program grew from 15 cadets to over 100. In October, 2013, he became the Recruiting Operations Officer for the Eagle Battalion Army ROTC program at Embry-Riddle Aeronautical University where he more than doubled the size of the program in six years. Cadet Command selected LTC McCulloch as the top recruiting officer out of 274 recruiters for 2019.

LTC McCulloch earned a Bachelor of Science Degree in History from Northern Illinois University in 1987 and a Master of Military Arts and Science Degree in History from the United States Army Command and General Staff College in 2002. He received thirty-one military service awards including the Bronze Star, eight Meritorious Service Medals and the Humanitarian Service Medal.

LTC McCulloch is married to the former Kelly Smyth of Wauconda, Illinois. They were married at Fort Sheridan, Illinois, in 1987. They have two children, Oakland Vincent McCulloch and Caileigh Nicholson. They also have a granddaughter, Ryleigh Jade Nicholson, and two grandsons, Christopher Bryce Nicholson and Oakland Maverick McCulloch.

Introduction

I've thought about writing a book for a long time. The idea for the content of this book initially came from the leadership lectures I've been giving since 2006. There is so much more to talk about than what I have time for in a typical one-hour lecture. This book is a compilation of the leadership lessons I have learned, practiced and taught to others.

When I took over as Professor of Military Science at the University of South Alabama in May, 2006, I started going around to high schools and colleges where I would speak to young men and women. I would always ask them what they wanted to be, and many of them told me they wanted to be leaders. When I asked what they meant by that and, more importantly, how they planned to become leaders, most of them gave me that deer-in-the-headlights look.

"If your actions inspire others to dream more, learn more, do more and become more, you are a leader."
-John Quincy Adams

Therefore, I decided to put together a presentation to help them understand what they needed to do to become good leaders. I immediately started getting invitations to speak. I delivered my presentation to high school and college students, adult groups, sports teams and businesses.

From as far back as I can remember, I have wanted to be a leader. In middle school and high school, I was always the captain of my sports teams. I was president of my class and president of our student council. As a college cadet at the United States Military Academy at West Point and in the Reserve Officer Training Corps (ROTC) at Northern Illinois University, I was always a leader and helped facilitate the training of other cadets. Once I received my commission as an officer in the United States Army, I spent 23 years as a leader. When I retired, I took up a leadership position in the civilian world as the associate director of a food bank. Now, once again, I'm a leader in the program dedicated to recruiting and training new cadets for the Army ROTC program at Embry-Riddle Aeronautical University. Being a leader, and teaching others to be leaders, are passions of mine. I believe it's every generation's responsibility to train the next generation of leaders – our replacements, if you will.

My last job as an active duty Army officer was Professor of Military Science at the University of South Alabama. Before I was selected to take over this Army ROTC program, I was one of the American foreign exchange instructors at the Australian Command and Staff College. Due to Australian laws, there can only be a certain number of foreign officers in country at any specific time. Therefore, when my replacement showed up, I had to leave the country within a month. Well, that did not line up with the timeline the Army had set for me to take over the ROTC program at the University of South Alabama. I received permission to show up three months before I was to take over the program. That turned out to be a blessing in disguise. I was able to observe how my predecessor ran the program. I got to know the people who were going to work for me, and I got a head start developing plans for how I wanted to lead the program.

One of the people working at the University of South Alabama when I arrived was an outstanding non-commissioned officer (NCO) named Master Sergeant David Powell. I quickly learned I could trust him, and I respected his opinions. Not only was he great at his job, but he was the kind of leader that always did things for the right reasons. One day Master Sergeant Powell and I were talking about the importance of what we were doing, namely training the future leaders of the United States Army and the future leaders of our great country. He said something I've never forgotten: "Great leadership handed down from generation to generation is what develops great nations."

You can replace the word nations with companies, organizations, teams, universities, hospitals or anything else you want, but it still rings true. I've always said, "Show me an organization with good leadership, and I'll show you a successful organization. Show me an organization with poor leadership, and I'll show you an organization that's struggling."

Since the day I had that conversation with Master Sergeant Powell, I have made it my life's mission to train as many future leaders as possible, whether for the Army or whatever professions they choose to join.

If you truly want to be a leader, my hope is that by reading this book you will gain some insights into the qualities required to be a good leader. If you are already in a position of leadership, then I hope reading this book will cause you to stop and reflect on how you are doing. It's possible for anybody to become a better leader. You owe it to yourself, as well as to the organizations and individuals you have the privilege and responsibility of leading, to become the leader you were meant to be.

Chapter 1

Defining Leadership

"Leadership is a potent combination of strategy and character. But if you must be without one, be without the strategy."
-Norman Schwarzkopf

AS I TRAVEL around and speak to different organizations, I always ask members of the audience to give me a definition of leadership. It amazes me how many people struggle to provide an answer. Leadership can be defined in many different ways. Warren Bennis, a pioneer in the contemporary field of Leadership Studies, noted, "To an extent, leadership is like beauty; it's hard to define, but you know it when you see it." Not everyone defines leadership the same way, and that's okay. However, if you want to be a leader, I would suggest the first thing you do is define what you believe leadership means. Once you can define leadership, only then can you determine the necessary steps to becoming a great leader.

What is Leadership?

Dictionary definitions of leadership are about as useful as dirty dishwater. *The New Oxford Dictionary of English* defines leadership as "The action of leading a group of people or an organization; the state or position of being a leader." The *Merriam-Webster Dictionary* defines leadership as "The office or position of a leader, the capacity to lead, and the act or instance of leading." Both definitions are true, but neither are very useful.

Other famous people have provided their own unique definitions.

Warren G. Bennis, American scholar and pioneer of Leadership Studies, said "Leadership is the capacity to translate vision into reality."

John W. Gardner, Secretary of Health, Education and Welfare under President Johnson, defined leadership as "The process of persuasion or example by which an individual (or leadership team) induces a group to pursue objectives held by the leader and his or her followers."

According to General Dwight D. Eisenhower, who led the

largest amphibious invasion in history, "Leadership is the art of getting someone else to do something you want done because he wants to do it."

I'm sure you can find a thousand definitions of leadership, but you need to formulate your definition of leadership. You need to find a definition that strikes a chord with you, that will drive your leadership style. Only then can you embark on the journey of becoming a better leader.

"A true leader has the confidence to stand alone, the courage to make tough decisions, and the compassion to listen to the needs of others. He does not set out to be a leader but becomes one by the equality of his actions and the integrity of his intent."
-Douglas MacArthur

For the purpose of this book we will use the United States Army's definition of leadership which says, "Leadership is the process of influencing people by providing purpose, direction and motivation while operating to accomplish a mission and improving the organization."

When I give lectures, I start with this definition of leadership. Quite often I can see reluctance in the eyes of the audience.

They're not sure they want to accept the Army's definition of leadership. When I explain this definition and why I believe it's important and relevant, many of those reluctant eyes begin to change. They tend to come around to my point of view.

I use this definition because it's what I know. I have been a leader in the Army for over 40 years. It's the standard by which I judge my own leadership capabilities and the standard that has proven successful over many decades.

I like this definition of leadership because it defines what leaders do as well as how and why they do things. The 'what' includes influencing people; the 'how' includes providing purpose, direction and motivation; the 'why' includes accomplishing a mission and improving the organization. These concepts have always seemed straightforward to me.

In my mind, this definition makes it easy to figure out the things you can do as a leader to improve your ability to accomplish the 'what' the 'how' and the 'why'.

I don't think this definition of leadership is much different from the way any Fortune 500 company would define leadership. They might change a few words here and there to fit their civilian language, but it's pretty much the same.

Even though I believe the Army's definition of leadership is superior to many others, I like to add a couple ideas to it. First, lead by example. Second, take care of the people on your team.

A great leader sets positive examples in all aspects of life. If you want people in your organization to act in certain ways, modeling good behavior is critical. You can encourage ethical and moral behaviors by conducting yourself in ethical and moral capacities. Leadership is not just a position or title. Leadership is action and example.

"Leadership is all about people. It is not about organizations. It is not about plans. It is not about strategies. It is all about people – motivating people to get the job done. You have to be people-oriented."
-Colin Powell

If you take care of the people in your organization, I believe they will take care of you. If you model ethical and moral behaviors, your people will do what you need them to do and expect them to do. I believe this because I have seen it in action time and time again.

Leadership is Leadership

I give leadership lectures to many different audiences. I speak to high school students, college students and athletic teams. I give presentations to faculty and staff at the universities where I work. I also speak to business leaders in the communities where I live and work. My presentations are usually well-received.

Occasionally I'll hear a comment like, "You only know about leadership in the military because that's where your leadership experience has been. You know nothing about leadership outside the military."

I'm amazed when someone says that to me. I can tell you that it's not true. One of the most important takeaways from my presentations and this book is simple: leadership is leadership. Period. It doesn't matter where you learned or practiced your leadership skills. Leadership is leadership. Leadership skills and experiences are transferable no matter which profession you join or which group you lead.

"Leadership is influence, nothing more, nothing less. Titles don't have much value when it comes to leading. True leadership cannot be awarded, appointed or assigned. It comes only from influence, and that cannot be mandated. It must be earned."
-John C. Maxwell

I know nothing about running a hospital. I actually try to avoid hospitals because there are mean doctors there who want to do bad things to me, like give me shots. I promise you, however, that if you put me in charge of a hospital tomorrow, I could run that hospital. Not only could I run it, but I could run it as well or better than the person currently running it. I am convinced of that because I know how to lead.

When I retired from the Army, I took a job as the deputy director of a large food bank that served counties in several states. My job as the deputy director was to conduct day-to-day operations of the food bank. Before I started there, I had no idea what a food bank did or how it operated. However, I set out to learn what I needed to understand and figured out the responsibilities of each team member. During the 18 months I was in charge of day-to-day operations, we increased the amount of food we distributed from 1.4 million pounds a year to 3.2 million pounds a year.

Leadership is leadership. Never let anyone tell you otherwise.

Key Take-aways

- Leaders set positive examples in everything they do every single day.
- Leadership skills and experience are transferrable.

Reflections

- Think of a time when you could have set a better example for the people in your organization.

- Think of a time when you could have better demonstrated just how much you care about a member of your team.

- Think of a time when you turned down a new leadership role in an area outside your comfort zone. Never be afraid to take on new leadership roles. Your skills and experiences are transferable and will help you be successful.

Professor of Military Science
University of South Alabama - 2006

First Salute Ceremony at Stetson University – 2011

With Kelly McCulloch
University High School Junior ROTC Military Ball - 2013

Notes

Chapter 2

It's Not About You; It's All About You

"When you were made a leader you weren't given a crown, you were given the responsibility to bring out the best in others."
-Jack Welch

BEING A LEADER is not easy, never has been, never will be. A good leader will have a huge impact on the lives of other people. A good leader will impact the success of organizations of all kinds. Understanding the concepts of what it takes to be a leader is not that difficult. Actually doing the things required of leaders, day in and day out, is another story. Thus, the dichotomy of this chapter and its title, *It's Not About You; It's All About You.*

I hope that by the end of this chapter you will understand that there are times when being a good leader is not about you and there are times when being a good leader is all about you. Until you understand this concept, believe it and live it, it will be difficult to lead.

It's Not About You

In the most critical sense, leadership, in almost every case, is not about you. Leadership is all about service, and I believe it's about selfless service. In order to be a good leader, you must first be a servant, a humble servant. Leaders with humility recognize they are no better or worse than other members of the team. A humble servant-leader will often be self-effacing in an effort to elevate other members of the team.

"Being humble means recognizing that we are not on earth to see how important we can become, but to see how much difference we can make in the lives of others."
-Gordon B. Hinckley

Being a leader is not about receiving better pay, living in a nicer house, driving a nicer car or receiving more privileges. Let's be honest, leaders often get some of those things, but that's not why true leaders want to lead, and it's certainly not why someone made you the leader. As a leader, you will be serving the ones who work for you or follow you as well as those for whom you work. The main goal of a good leader will be to make the organization and its people better each and every day.

Every time I commission a new second lieutenant in the United States Army, I give them a little speech during their ceremony. I tell them, "Enjoy today, because today is all about you." Then I tell them, "As a leader, today is the last day that is all about you. From now on, it will be about your subordinates, your boss, your unit, the mission, the Army and the country. Then, if we have time, we can talk about you."

"Always remember that leadership is a privilege. When you are in a leadership role, your influence may affect the trajectories of people's entire careers and often their lives!"
-Bill Treasurer

Sometimes leaders are required to make choices and do things that are not in their best interest. They'll be required to do things that are in the best interest of the organization or the people for whom they are responsible. When I was a company commander, I had a very toxic subordinate leader in my unit. He was beating his wife, borrowing money from his subordinates and writing bad checks all over town. He had also been convicted of driving under the influence. Not exactly the type of leader who was setting a good example for his soldiers. I decided I was going to discharge him from his position. However, he had already served for 17 years and my boss at the time did not want me to do this. He told me, "That soldier has spent 17 years in the Army and deserves the right to retire from the Army."

I said, "No soldier has the right to retire. Retirement is earned, and I'm going to remove him." After a long discussion, my boss told me that if I pursued this course of action it would reflect in my Officer Evaluation Report (OER). I told him I was sticking with my decision and he could do what he thought he must in relation to my OER. I did what I knew was right and discharged the soldier from active duty. My boss, true to his word, made sure it was reflected in my OER.

That OER certainly had a lot to do with the way my career went from that point forward. I know it affected future promotions and positions. However, I made the best choice for the organization at the time, not the choice that was best for me in the long run. Even though it certainly affected my career, I would do the same thing over again. I can look in the mirror every morning and be satisfied that the decision I made was the right decision for the organization. That is what good leaders do. They put the good of the organization before their own well-being. It's not always easy, but good leaders make those types of decisions and those kinds of personal sacrifices.

One of my favorite quotes goes like this: "If service is below you, then leadership is beyond you." If you are not willing to internalize this concept, stop reading this book right now. Until you understand this concept, it will be difficult to become the leader you were meant to be.

It's All About You

Just because you have the title of leader does not necessarily mean you are the leader. That is something you must earn, and you will have to earn it all day, every day. In reality, you are not the leader until the people you lead decide you are the leader. The world is full of people who have the title of leader; many of them don't actually lead.

Setting the Example

As a leader, the things you do and the actions you take are daily examples to those you lead. It's naïve to think that the people you lead or the people who work for you aren't watching you. They are. You are being watched in everything you do every day.

For example, if you are supposed to work until 5:00 p.m. but you leave at 4:45 p.m., the people who work for you will notice. They will undoubtedly say to themselves, "If the boss can leave 15 minutes early, why can't we?" If you walk past a piece of trash on the floor and don't stop to pick it up and throw it away, how can you expect the people who work for you to do the same?

My father used to tell me, "If you say one thing but do something else, it will be your actions that are believed." Being a leader is all about deeds, not words. Recently, I attended an event where I heard a great story. The main speaker, a man named Jonathan Fanning, told about a mother who brought her diabetic son to visit Ghandi. The mother and son travelled a long way to meet with him. The son respected Gandhi and she thought this was her last chance to save him. However, when they met with Gandhi and she asked him to tell her son not to eat sugar, Ghandi said, " Come back in two weeks."

"Leadership is not about titles, positions or flow charts; it is about one life influencing another."
-John C. Maxwell

The mother, thinking about the distance they had traveled, was not happy with that answer. She could not understand why Gandhi wouldn't just tell her son not to eat sugar. In two weeks, they came back and again met with Gandhi. He said to the young man, "Stop eating sugar."

The mother said, " Why couldn't you have told my son two weeks ago to stop eating sugar?"

Gandhi replied, "Two weeks ago I was still eating sugar." Deeds, not words. Never ask someone to do something you're not willing to do yourself. It's not easy, but it's so very powerful, and it's what good leaders do – they always lead by example.

Every time you do something, you are setting a new standard. You will either raise the bar or lower the bar. The choice is yours. Good leaders practice self-discipline in order to make sure they are setting examples they want others to follow, not just occasionally but each and every day. Far too often today, leaders say one thing but do something else, usually to better their own self-interests instead of the interests of their people or organizations. My father had many bad habits. I must admit, however, that I am the man I am today in large part due to him. I learned many things from him. I learned about things I should do, and I learned about things I should never do. One of those negative lessons was based on something he once told me. He said, "Do as I say, not as I do." If you want to be a good leader, you won't have that luxury. One of your most important jobs as a leader is to inspire everyone you lead to want to be like you. The only way you can do that is by striving to set good examples in all that you do each and every day.

As a leader, you'll have an incredible opportunity to inspire and change the lives of other people. Good leaders won't take that opportunity for granted.

No Vacations from Being the Leader

You are a leader 24 hours a day, 7 days a week, 365 days a year. You don't get to take vacations from being the leader. That doesn't mean you can't take vacations; it means you are never *not* the leader. Even when you are on vacation, you are still the leader.

"Earn your leadership every day."
-Michael Jordan

I don't know how many times in my career I've been on vacation with my family when I've received a phone call from one of my personnel saying, "Boss, I know you're on vacation, but we have an issue and we could use your input."

At that point, I would tell my wife and kids to go do whatever it is wives and kids do on vacation and I would deal with the problem. After I dealt with the problem, I would go back to being a husband and a dad on vacation with his family. Good leaders understand and embrace the fact there are some small prices to pay when in a position of leadership.

Being the Moral Compass

As a leader, you are the moral, ethical and lawful compass of your organization. I always tell my listeners that the people who work for them are like their children. They will do what they are allowed to do. If you let them do bad things, they will do bad things. If you hold them to high standards and encourage them to do good things, they will do good things.

When I was a senior lieutenant, I took over the mortar platoon in our battalion and had to do an inventory of the equipment. Once finished, I discovered we were missing a set of binoculars. During one of the first meetings with my subordinate leaders, I explained to them the importance of finding those binoculars because we needed them to do our job correctly.

Every organization has a person that I call the scrounger. You know, that person who can find or get anything the organization needs. I knew who the scrounger was in my unit.

A couple days after the meeting, I walked into my office and found a pair of binoculars sitting on my desk. In the Army every piece of equipment is identified by a serial number. I checked the serial number and quickly figured out that those were not our binoculars. They belonged to some other unit. When I asked my scrounger where he got the binoculars, he said, "Boss, you don't want to know."

I said, "Take them back to where you found them."

"Boss," he said, "you told us how important it was to find our binoculars so we can do our job."

"Yes," I said, "I told you it was important to find *our* binoculars, not somebody else's."

What kind of message would I have sent to my soldiers if I

had kept those binoculars? That it was okay to steal something from another unit as long as we benefitted?

Leaders are the moral compass of their organizations. Leaders do what is right, no matter the situation, even if there may be no personal benefit. Even when nobody else is watching. Setting good examples is critical when trying to get people to follow. Set high standards, keep them yourself, and your subordinates will follow suit. Given the choice, many people will do less than they need to do. Good leaders don't allow their followers that choice. They demand high standards and model the behaviors that will lead to achieving those standards.

"The quality of a leader is reflected in the standards they set for themselves."
-Ray Kroc

One of my favorite quotes is by Alexis de Tocqueville. He said, "America is great because America is good, and if America ever ceases to be good, America will cease to be great." I believe this to be true, not just for America, but for every organization. Too many organizations in too many arenas – politics, education, business, religion, sports, military – have been making unsound and unwise decisions. Good leaders will step up to the challenges of making decisions that benefit their organizations even at the expense of their own personal interests.

Key Take-aways

- Being a leader is not easy. Remember, it's not about you, yet it's all about you.

- Great leaders understand leadership is all about people.

- Leaders will always set good examples for their team.

Reflections

- Take an honest look at your leadership style. Are you a leader who makes decisions that are in your best interests, or are you a leader who makes decisions that put the interests of your people and organization first?

- If you are not practicing selfless service as a leader, what changes could you make?

Speaking at Commissioning Ceremony
Stetson University - 2011

Giving instructions to soon-to-be Lieutenant Ethan Wagnon
at Commissioning Ceremony, Stetson University - 2013

Notes

Chapter 3

A Leader is Comfortable Being in Charge

"A leader must be self-confident and must possess imagination."
-Omar N. Bradley

ANY LEADER WILL want to make an organization better than it was before he or she arrived. It's one of the most important goals a leader can have. Positive change in an organization will not happen by accident. As a leader, you have to make it happen. It's not always easy, but the reason somebody put you in a position of leadership was to make things happen.

Leaders Have a Vision and a Plan

In order to make an organization better, a good leader will determine a starting point by identifying where an organization is at and then setting measurable short-term and long-term goals for improvement. This takes vision, planning and execution. What do you want the organization to look like a month from now, a year from now, five years from now, ten years from now? Given the uncertainties at any time in the world, this is not always easy. However, with correct planning and unwavering belief, you can influence the future of your organization and maybe change the way the entire industry looks going forward.

"The very essence of leadership is that you have to have vision. You can't blow an uncertain trumpet."
-Theodore Hesburgh

Once you have a vision in place and a plan to execute that vision, you can communicate to your people why you want to move the organization to a new place and how you plan to do it. If you think you can do it by yourself, you're mistaken. The people you lead will be the ones that execute your plan and help make your vision a reality.

When I took over the ROTC program at the University of South Alabama, I had to attend a two-week course at Fort

Monroe, Virginia. At that time, Fort Monroe was the headquarters for Cadet Command, which is the organization that controls all Army ROTC programs. All the Professors of Military Science from across the country who were taking charge of Army ROTC programs had to attend this course. One of the admirable things about the Army is that when they promote you to a new position of responsibility, they will send you to a school that teaches you the information you'll need to be successful at that position.

During the two-week course I attended, we had the honor of having the commander of the entire program, Major General Winfield, speak to us. I had worked with Major General Winfield at Fort Knox, Kentucky, in the 194th Separate Armored Brigade when he was a lieutenant colonel and I was a captain. Unlike the rest of my companions, I had some understanding of his philosophies and was familiar with his beliefs and the expectations he had of people who worked for him. He spoke for an hour. I honestly don't remember everything he talked about. However, one thing he said to us hit home and stuck in my mind. He said, "If you are taking over an Army ROTC program that is not meeting its mission goal of commissioning the target number of lieutenants each year, then you should lie awake at night thinking about how you are going to fix your program."

I was one of those Professors of Military Science who was

about to take over just such a program. The Army ROTC program at the University of South Alabama had not made its mission in seven years. Therefore, that evening I went back to my room and started to figure out what I could do to fix the problem. After dinner, I pulled out a 3 x 5 index card and started writing down what I thought it would take to fix the program I was about to lead.

The Army ROTC program I was taking over had 53 cadets enrolled at the time. The first thing I did was write down my primary goal on that index card. I wrote, "At the end of my three years as Professor of Military Science, I will have 150 cadets and triple the size of the program." I knew it was an audacious goal, but I believed we could make it happen.

"Vision without action is merely a dream. Action without vision just passes the time. Vision with action can change the world."
-Joel A. Baker

I then wrote down how I was going to accomplish that goal in three years. The first thing I wrote was simple, "Take care of my cadets." I figured it did no good to get cadets to join the program if we did not take care of them once they were there. If we, the cadre, did not take care of the cadets, they would leave the program and join some other organization that would take care of them and help them. Many people helped me through the commissioning process when I went through Army ROTC a hundred years ago. Now it was my turn to help as many of these young men and women as possible through the same process.

The second thing I wrote to ensure we could meet that goal was, "Set good examples every day." I knew the young men and women who had decided to join Army ROTC were looking for a way of life, a way to serve their country, a way to become leaders. I figured the best way to show them was to set good examples for them every day by my words and my actions. I would explain to them and then demonstrate myself how an Army officer spoke, dressed and interacted with others.

By the way, I still have that card. It sits on my desk to remind me why I do what I do.

Leaders Communicate a Vision and a Plan to Their Employees

Once you have your vision in place and a specific plan of action to reach your goals, then you can communicate that vision and plan to the people who work for you. Again, if you think you can get your organization from where it is today to where you want it to be all by yourself, you are mistaken. The people you lead will bring your vision to life.

After I crystalized my vision, set goals and developed a plan of action to reach those goals, I told my boss, whose office was

345 miles away in Huntsville, Alabama. He just laughed and told me there was no way I could accomplish that in three years. I told him that not only could we reach that goal, but that we absolutely would reach that goal before I left my position there. I also told him that when we did reach that goal he would owe me two things. The first one was a selfish request. I told him he would owe me a steak dinner at Café 316, my favorite restaurant. The second request was for my cadre and my cadets. I told him he would have to come to the University of South Alabama and do physical training (PT) with my cadets. He agreed to both.

I returned to the university after my two-week course. Immediately after I took over as Professor of Military Science I had my first staff meeting with the cadre, my team. I explained to them my overall goal for the program, why I had set that goal and how we were going to reach that goal. The last thing I told them during that staff meeting was what I expected from each of them. I made sure they understood that not only would I be asking certain things of them, I'd be demanding things of them. I also gave them the opportunity and responsibility to ask questions when they did not understand my vision and plan.

I told them I expected each of them to set good examples for the cadets every day. I included myself in that request. I told them that, in turn, I would be responsible for setting good examples for them. I said, "The reason you are here and the reason the Army pays you is to take care of the cadets in this program." I made it clear that if they failed in this basic responsibility, they would not be able to work for me. I emphasized that we could not grow the program unless we took care of the cadets. To make sure they understood this mandate, I had each of them say it out loud.

A couple weeks later, I was walking down the hall past the office of a cadre member. As I passed by, one of my cadets knocked on his door. I glanced in the office and saw that my employee had his feet on his desk. He was talking on his cell phone and drinking a Coke. I heard him tell the cadet, "I'm busy, come back tomorrow." As the cadet turned to leave, I told him to go take a seat in the waiting area and I would assist him in a few minutes.

I turned around and was about to ask my employee what he thought he was doing. Instead, I went back to my office where I made a couple of phone calls. I called my boss and the contractor representative and let them both know I was going to dismiss this employee as well as the reasons behind my decision. They both supported my decision. I took out a piece of paper, wrote down a few things, returned to this man's office and let him read what I had written. I told him to pack his stuff and get out. "You're fired," I told him. "You no longer work here."

He said, "You can't fire me."

"I just did," I replied. I reminded him that I had made it perfectly clear from day one that the only reason he worked for this organization was to take care of the cadets. Since he had failed to do that, he could no longer work for me. How many more times do you think I had to deal with this issue at the University of South Alabama? That's right. Just that once. Everyone else figured out that I wasn't kidding. After that incident, each of the other cadre members made it their number one priority to take care of the cadets enrolled in the program.

Once the cadre member that I fired had collected his things, given me his keys and left the building, I called the young cadet into my office. I helped him work through some issues he was having, and he graduated as a commissioned second lieutenant three years later. Would he have stayed in the program and been commissioned if we had not helped him right then? Maybe, maybe not.

"When you set standards and stick to them, there will be people who fall away. Let them."
-Ralph Waldo Emerson

When I handed the program over to the next Professor of Military Science three years later, we had 179 cadets in the program. We had more than tripled the size of the program in three years. He did not have to worry about taking over a program that was not going to make its mission.

To the credit of my boss, a man named Colonel Eli Ballard, he kept his end of the agreement. He traveled to Mobile and spent the night at my house. He took me out to my favorite restaurant where I had a delicious steak dinner on him. He then got up the next morning and went to physical training with my cadets. He took them on a long run, and let me tell you, Colonel Ballard could run! He then gave the cadets a very inspiring speech at the end of the run. Over the years, he did so much more than that to help our program and our cadets. He gave us more scholarship money and any extra equipment we requested. He came down and gave a motivating speech at the graduation program where we commissioned nine second lieutenants that year. Colonel Ballard was the epitome of what a leader should be, and I feel fortunate to have had the opportunity to work for him.

When you assume leadership of an organization, do an analysis of where your organization is at that point and then figure out where you want to take that organization. Develop a plan to get your organization from where it currently is to where you want it to be in the future. Communicate the goals to your employees to make sure they understand your expectations. I promise you it works. You and your organization can accomplish amazing things!

Leaders Are Decisive

I'm sure none of you reading this book has ever been in an organization where the leader could not make a decision, right? The reality is, we've all had leaders in our lives that fit that description. How did that indecisiveness affect your organization? How did that type of leader affect you personally?

When a leader cannot or will not make decisions that need to be made, it causes the people in that organization to have doubts, not just about the leader, but about the organization. A leader who cannot or will not make decisions causes frustration and confusion in the organization. If you want to be a good leader, it's important to be decisive and make the tough decisions.

"In any moment of decision the best thing you can do is the right thing, the next best thing is the wrong thing, and the worst thing you can do is nothing."
-Theodore Roosevelt

When asked to evaluate an organization, I often find that one of the problems is the inability of its leader to make timely decisions. When confronted as to why decisions aren't made, I often hear the same answer. "I did not have all the information I needed to make a decision." Well, guess what? The world where a leader will always have all the information needed to make timely decisions is called a perfect world, and that world doesn't exist.

General George S. Patton, Jr., one of the greatest leaders this country has ever produced, once said, "A good plan violently executed now is better than a perfect plan executed next week." I realize that many of the people reading this book are not or will not be leaders in the military, so the word 'violently' may not pertain to you. However, you can easily change the word 'violently' to 'vigorously' without changing the essence of the quote.

I am not advocating the execution of sub-standard plans. What I'm saying, and what I believe, is that a good leader will act when a decision is required.

In the real world, you'll never have all the information you'd like to have in order to make all important decisions. In the real world, you take the information you have, make an educated guess on the information you don't know and make a decision. You can always make detours and changes along the way as more information becomes available. However, if you do not make a decision and start on the journey that is required, you will waste valuable time and your organization and its people will suffer.

Another factor that often prevents leaders from making decisions is their aversion to risk. If you are risk averse, you may need to find some other position; leadership may not be for you. I'm not saying you should be reckless, but a good leader is willing to take risks. The key is to know the difference between a risk and a gamble when making decisions. There's a big difference between risk-taking and gambling. In risk-taking, you have considered the potential consequences of your choices and can anticipate contingency actions. In gambling, you are guessing and don't have real control of the potential outcome.

Field Marshall Erwin Rommel, a brilliant leader in World War II, once said, "The difference between a risk and a gamble is simple. If you take a risk and fail, you can recover from it. If you take a gamble and fail, you cannot recover from it."

Leaders make tough decisions. As a leader, if you are unable or unwilling to make decisions, the people who work for you will lose confidence in you. Good leaders are decisive, willing to take risks and are not afraid to make decisions. We pay leaders to make decisions. Be a decisive leader!

Change

Leaders embrace change. I can readily admit that this is not always the strongest part of my leadership style. I'm comfortable with some types of change, but I've been resistant to changes in some areas – technology, for example. There have been times when my wife, Kelly, has had to remind me that change is not always bad. In the end, she's usually right. Okay, she's always right. A good leader can't be afraid of making changes. Anytime I talk about this topic, I remind people of the quote by the Greek philosopher Heraclitus: "The only thing that is constant is change."

Maybe someone selected you to lead an organization specifically to make changes. Maybe the organization is failing. Maybe it's broken. Maybe it's doing something illegal.

During my career there have been several times when I've been put in charge of a specific organization for the sole purpose of making changes to that organization. In one of those cases, my boss said, "If you do things the same way things have always been done, you will continue to get the same results."

"Change is the law of life and those who look only to the past or present are certain to miss the future."
-John F. Kennedy

In one such case, my boss put me in charge of an Improved TOW Vehicle (ITV) platoon. For anyone who knows anything about the military, I am now dating myself. That weapon system no longer exists, nor has it for many years. This ITV was a TOW missile system mounted on a M113 chassis. The reason my boss put me in charge of that platoon was because things needed to be changed. With the introduction of the Bradley Infantry Vehicle, which also had a mounted TOW weapon system, the ITV units were becoming obsolete. During unit rotations to the

National Training Center, where units took part in simulated battles, some ITV units would not fire a single shot.

I knew something had to be changed. The first thing I did was make sure I learned everything there was to know about that weapon system. I dug into doctrine. I researched the mechanics and maintenance of the vehicle and weapon system. I spent time learning about the areas where I thought changes needed to occur to make that weapon system viable again on the battlefield. Then I dug into how we trained gunnery skills.

The Army designed this weapon system to sit in one place, in a defensive position, so it could engage targets as they approached. However, since the Army introduced this weapon system, the military had changed its doctrine to one that was more offensively oriented. Since I could not change the weapon system itself, I had to change the way that it engaged a target.

I concluded that if we wanted to make the ITV a viable weapon system on the battlefield, we needed to make changes in how we trained our gunnery crews. Consequently, I developed a new program to train our crews and gunners. I spent months speaking with my soldiers in order to convince them that this new system of training was the right answer. We then ran our crews through this new gunnery training, not just once as required by training standards, but multiple times until they became comfortable.

When our battalion deployed to the National Training Center

at Fort Irwin a few months later, the results were nothing short of amazing. Not only did we do well, we broke all the records for the number of kills any ITV platoon had ever made in any rotation to the National Training Center. That new method of training gunnery became the standard for all ITV platoons in the 24th Infantry Division.

My boss knew changes to the ITV platoon had to occur if we wanted that weapon system to be viable on the battlefield. Therefore, he put me in charge to make those changes. Change was necessary, and I convinced my soldiers of that. The results spoke for themselves.

"The secret of change is to focus all of your energy, not on fighting the old, but on building the new."
-Socrates

I don't believe in change just for the sake of change. That sort of change is rarely good for an organization or its people. Most of the time, changes that are made just for the sake of change are done to stroke the ego of whoever is in charge. A good leader will figure out what things are working for an organization, leave those things alone and then change things that are not working.

I do not like to change a bunch of things right away. When I take over as the leader of an organization, I like to get to know the organization before I make any changes. Unless, of course, the organization is completely broken or doing things that are illegal. Those things should be changed right away. I generally like to walk around to see what's going on. I talk to the workers and ask their opinions about how things are going. I like to get a feeling for what is working and what is not working. Based on those observations, I can evaluate the organization fairly and figure out what kinds of changes need to be made, if any.

One of the most important questions I ask people is, "Why are you doing things this way?"

The answer is often the same. "Because that's the way we've always done it."

When someone says this, I want to bang my head against the wall. In my opinion, it's not a good answer. It's an answer that often belies laziness. I'd much rather hear somebody say, "That's the way we've always done it and it works because…"

When I ask people that question, I am honestly interested in their professional opinions. I want to know why things work and, yet, I also want to know if there are better ways to do the jobs.

There is one thing I always do immediately when I take a new position. The night before I take over an organization, my wife and I will go in and hang all my things on the walls of my new office. I need her help because she knows what looks good and what doesn't. If the desk is facing one way, then it will be facing a different way the next day when my team members come into the office. I want everyone to know that there's a new person in charge. One of the easiest ways to convey that message is to change the office and make it my own.

There is a difference between managing change and implementing change. As a leader, if you are only managing change, you're already behind the power curve. If you are only managing change, someone else is probably dictating what changes need to be made.

"People at the top of organizations have all the power and no knowledge. People at the bottom have all the knowledge and none of the power. Until people at the top relinquish power to those at the bottom – no organization can operate at maximum efficiency."
-Simon Sinek

A good leader should be able to see what changes need to occur and implement them before someone forces changes on the organization. Don't get me wrong, I know there are good idea fairies in every organization. We've all had bosses that will occasionally come up with good ideas and will direct the implementation of those ideas. However, a good leader will see what changes an organization needs and make them happen before someone else directs those changes.

When I was a lieutenant, I had the honor of working for Major Joseph Martz. He eventually became Lieutenant General Martz before he retired from the Army and was one of the best leaders with whom I ever had the privilege of serving. He once told me, "Trying to manage change is dangerous. Be the person who dictates change and you will be in control of the direction your organization is going."

Implementing change in an organization is never easy. Most organizations have a collective memory of "how things have always been done" and are resistant to change. The people of any organization are creatures of habit and like to do things the same way they've always done them. As a leader, you should understand that change is constant and necessary if you want your organization to stay on top. Just as important as understanding that changes are necessary to keep your organization at the forefront of your profession, a good leader will help all members of the team understand that change is necessary and good for both them and the organization. After all, any time you make changes, the first thing a team member will ask is, "How will this affect me?" Remember, good leaders will get the team to buy into the decisions they make.

Key Take-aways

- A good leader will develop a vision and plan for where the organization will go.

- If you want to lead, you must be ready to step up, take charge and implement change.

- Leaders are not afraid to make tough decisions.

Reflections

- Figure out effective ways to communicate to the team where your organization is today and where you want the organization to be in the future. Then figure out how to get there.

- Have there ever been times when you were not decisive? In the future, have the courage to make important decisions, even when you do not have all the information. Be ready to adapt as circumstances dictate.

- Have there been times in the past when you did not take full responsibility for something in your organization? Remember, the buck stops with you. Accept the responsibilities that come with leadership. Figure out ways to give credit where credit is due when your team is successful and take responsibility when your team is not.

Commissioning Ceremony for Second Lieutenant
Robert Brown - 2014

Eight newly commissioned second lieutenants
Stetson University - 2018

Notes

Chapter 4

A Leader Communicates

"Congress can make a general, but only communication can make him a commander."
-Omar N. Bradley

A LEADER COMMUNICATES. It's what leaders do. As I travel around speaking to people about leadership, I emphasize how important it is for leaders to be good communicators. If you want to be a great leader, communicating with others is critically important. I'm talking about all forms of communication, whether verbal, written or non-verbal.

Developing Communication Skills

It doesn't matter if you are speaking to one person in the privacy of your office or speaking in front of large groups of people, a good leader will be comfortable speaking with and to others. When you speak, people will judge your communication skills. They will check to see if you are confident in what you are saying. If you are confident, it's more likely your audience will believe what you are saying. If you are nervous and do not speak well, it's more likely your audience will have doubts about what you are telling them.

"Communication is a skill that you can learn. It's like riding a bicycle or typing. If you're willing to work at it, you can rapidly improve your communication skills."
-Brian Tracy

When I tell people who want to be leaders that at some point they will have to speak in front of groups, I often hear, "Oh, I could never do that!"

I respond with two answers. "First," I'll say, "if you really can't get up in front of people and speak, it's doubtful you'll be able to lead." Then I'll say, "Second, I believe that you *can* get up in front of people and speak if you really want to be a leader."

There are all kinds of tricks people use to feel comfortable while standing in front of a crowd and speaking to them. I've been doing public speaking events for so long now that I don't even blink at getting up in front of a crowd anymore. Here is what I've done myself and also shared with others:

Even though you're addressing an entire audience when speaking, that doesn't mean you have to engage every single person in the audience. When I begin a presentation, I start by speaking to the center of the group. Then I scan to the left and scan back to the right. While I do this, I pay attention to as many people in the group as possible. It's easy to see if the audience is engaged and interested. It's important to identify individual members of the audience who seem particularly eager to listen. I zero in on those people frequently while I'm speaking during the rest of the presentation. Those individuals are also the ones I will try to engage in examples or later during questions and answers. I still scan the entire audience but identify and engage with a few intent listeners. This has always helped me feel comfortable during a presentation and can work for you as well.

I always have one of the cadets from the Army ROTC program at Stetson University act as the master of ceremonies at commissioning events. I do this not only to help develop their communication and leadership skills, but also because it's important that the cadets take ownership of their program.

I give the chosen cadet the script for the ceremony at least seven days before the event. I tell whoever is going to be the MC that they need to read the script aloud a couple dozen times before the ceremony. I tell them the first dozen times to read the script aloud in front of a mirror. Then, the last couple times they practice the script, they should read it in front of a few people, preferably people who might be able to offer critical yet constructive criticism. The cadets need to feel comfortable with what's in the script. They must feel confident that they will be able to pronounce all the words and, more importantly, all the names correctly. By practicing in front of people, the cadets will learn how to pace the presentation and not feel rushed. I tell them, "If you think your delivery is too slow, it's not. Slow down even more." Then I remind them that nobody else knows what's in the script so if they make a mistake, keep going. Act like that's what you were supposed to say. No one will know the difference unless they let everyone in on the fact that a mistake was made. Own the script and the delivery of the message and people will believe what you are telling them.

As a leader, you will not always have the luxury of being able to read from a script. There will be times when you must get in front of people and give a presentation, lecture or speech without a script to follow. You'll be more convincing if you can deliver a presentation without a script and if you are not standing behind a podium. Any time I see someone who gives a presentation, lecture or speech from behind a podium I suspect that person is scared or nervous. Whether that conclusion is true or not, I believe it's the perception many people have.

When I'm asked to give a presentation, lecture or speech, I approach the preparation for each of them in the same manner. The first thing I do is write the presentation out word for word. I write it just as I want to deliver it. Then I read the material over and over until I have memorized what I want to say. If I'll be giving this presentation without slides, I'll write key points of my talk on 3 x 5 note cards. Most of the time I don't look at the cards during my talk, but it's nice to have them available just in case I need them. Nobody's perfect. If I'll be using a slideshow with the presentation, I develop the slides after I've written the text of the presentation.

When it comes to using slides in a presentation, it's important to remember a few key points. First, the fewer the better. Less is more. Second, only put bullet points on your slides. Don't make them too wordy with long, complete sentences. Remember, the slides are there for two reasons: to keep you on track and to help the audience follow along. I have found that using slides during a presentation helps keep my audience engaged. Keep the slides simple, easy to follow and pleasant to look at. Then, practice the presentation repeatedly until you can give it in a confident and polished manner. I give three different lectures on a regular basis. I tell people that I've given those lectures so many times that I could probably deliver them in my sleep, and I may have a couple times.

A good leader will learn to write well. This form of communication is the one people have most difficulty with today. People today just don't write as much as folks used to. It's a lost art form for the most part. All forms of communication – letters, evaluations, emails, texts – that a leader writes should be clear and concise, grammatically correct, easy to read and easy to understand. If people have to re-read several times what you've written, you've failed to communicate effectively through your writing.

The act of writing is no different than any other type of exercise. The more you do it, the stronger you get. President Lincoln once said, "No speech is finished until it is given." Lincoln would keep re-writing a speech until he actually delivered it. The Gettysburg Address had notes in the margins because he continued to work on the speech while listening to the speakers before him. Lincoln always felt a speaker should look for ways to say more with fewer words. Make your words impactful, and always look for shorter ways to say things.

While I understand that shorthand is the way a lot of people communicate these days, especially via email and text, I feel that sending messages in complete, grammatically correct sentences reflects on your overall professionalism. "R U coming?" Is it really that much more difficult to write, "Are you coming?"

When I receive shorthand texts or emails, it tells me that the person sending them doesn't fully understand the importance of good communication. It tells me that the person may not grasp the boss-employee relationship. A good leader will write well and demand that others do the same. Your written communication is a reflection of you as a person and as a leader. Take the time to write effectively and properly and ask the same of your employees. It will enhance the way others view you as a leader.

A good leader is cognizant of body language when speaking with others. People who see you speak and watch how you conduct yourself and interact with other people can tell a lot about what kind of leader you are by observing your body language.

Last year I visited 30 high schools and spoke to over 5,000 students. Usually, it meant that I would be at a school for up to seven hours. I would typically speak to each class of Junior ROTC cadets throughout the day. When I got home, I would often tell my wife that I felt like I had been beaten with a baseball bat. Why did I feel that way when all I had done was talk to kids? Well, it wasn't just the speaking. It was also that I was on display the entire day. Young men and women were watching me continually. They watched my facial expressions, how I stood, how I moved my arms and hands and much more. They watched how I interacted with their fellow students when I was answering questions.

All of these non-verbal communications skills are important, sometimes just as important as your speaking skills. People who watch you speak will notice if you are comfortable in front of them. They can tell if you believe what you're saying. They will notice if you are there to truly help them and answer their questions. They will notice if you look like a leader. By that I mean standing tall and appearing clean-cut and confident. A good leader won't neglect these important aspects of communication. They are important and they matter to others.

Communication in Your Organization

Every so often, friends who are in charge of various organizations will ask me to spend a day or two looking at how they do things. Usually they ask me to do this because the organization is having issues and they need a fresh set of eyes to look at how things are done. Since I believe that every organization has areas where they can make improvements, I am always happy to spend a few days with them and share my opinions on where I think there is room for improvement.

"The single biggest problem in communication is the illusion that it has taken place."
-George Bernard Shaw

The first thing I typically review is the strength of communication within the organization. What I have found is that communication in many organizations is not as good as its leaders and workers think it is. As I talk to people, I'll ask as many as I can this simple question, "How good is the communication in your organization?"

A lot of people answer, "Great!"

My first thought when I hear this is usually, "I doubt that or I wouldn't be here." Show me an organization that communicates well and I will show you a successful organization. Show me an organization that does not communicate well and I will show you an organization that is struggling.

A good leader can improve an organization's communication on many different levels. These improvements will impact people inside and outside the organization.

One of the first things I tell leaders is that if they want to improve their organization's communication they should teach everybody in the organization to regularly ask one simple question: Who else needs to know? Any time there's new information obtained by a member of the team, the person should ask that question. Who else needs to know this? It sounds simple, but it's paramount to effective communication.

I can't tell you how many times I've given someone who worked for me a task that I needed them to accomplish along with a deadline. Every week or so, I would conduct an in-progress review to check on the progress of the project. I'd simply ask an employee, "Where are you on the project?"

In more cases than I can remember, the team member would say, "I have accomplished these things, but I'm still missing this information in order to complete the project." This can go on for weeks.

More often than not, somebody else in the organization has the information needed by the other person to complete the task at hand. They simply didn't realize that the information they possessed needed to be shared. If they had shared what they knew in a timely manner, the person assigned to the job could have finished it successfully in a much more timely fashion.

Believe it or not, this happens all the time in many organizations. As a leader, it's important to eliminate this communication block or at least keep it to a minimum. In my many years of leadership, I've found the best way to do this is by teaching everybody in the organization that every time they find out new information they should ask themselves, "Who else needs to know?"

As easy as this sounds, I also can tell you that sometimes there are people in an organization who don't want this to happen. I call them the 'knowledge is power' brokers. They are the people in an organization who believe that with knowledge comes power and if they control all the knowledge, they will be considered indispensable.

As a leader, it's important to be able to recognize who these power brokers are because they can harm an organization and keep it from its mission. They are like a cancer in an organization, but not all of them are irredeemable. A good leader will coach people like this into becoming good team members. However, if you can't convince them to get on board with the sharing of important information, they should be removed or your organization will never be as efficient and successful as it could be.

When I took over as the associate director of a local food bank, my job was to oversee day-to-day operations of the organization. I quickly figured out I had one of these power brokers working for me at the food bank. She had worked there for 32 years and knew more about how the organization accomplished things than anyone else. She probably had forgotten things that the rest of us had not even thought of. I tried very hard to get her to change, but she kept resisting any changes. She was purposely unwilling to share information with other employees that would help them accomplish their jobs.

In the end, I realized I needed to dismiss her from the organization. At one point, I hired a new employee, a young man who was an enterprising person and a hard worker. To test my theory about what this power broker was doing, I went into her office before one of our staff meetings and during a casual conversation, relayed to her some information that only she and I would know. It was information that the new employee would have found useful to do his job effectively. Sure enough, when I assigned him the task he was supposed complete, she never said a word. She did not offer to share any of the information that I had given her, even though she knew he needed it to do his job.

Over the next few weeks, during our staff meetings, I would ask the young man how the project was coming. He would answer by updating me on the progress he had made but inevitably would tell me that he was missing some important information that would allow him to finish the job. Each time he said this, I would look at the power broker hoping she would volunteer to share the information with him. She never did. Finally, I gave the young man the information he needed to complete his task.

After the staff meeting, I informed the director of the food bank that I was going to let this employee go. I walked back to my office, took out a piece of paper and wrote down a few things. I walked into my power broker's office and put the piece of paper on her desk. I told her I was terminating her employment at the food bank and that she could clean out her desk, pack her things and leave. She quickly replied that I couldn't fire her because she knew more than anyone else who worked there. I told her I was aware of that and that this was a difficult decision, but she was fired and she would have to leave. It took us a while to figure out everything she did, but after we did, our organization ran much more efficiently.

Communication is a Two-way Street

When I talk about communication inside an organization, I always emphasize that communication is a two-way street. Communication is not just the leader telling people what to do. A good leader will listen to what other people in the organization have to say. If your leadership style embraces only top down communication, you're merely a boss instead of a true leader. At worst, you could be considered a dictator.

Throughout my career as a leader, whether in the Army or at the food bank, I had to make many decisions every day. One of the ways I ensured communication remained a two-way street in my organization was by using the following simple method: anytime I needed to make a decision, I would call my junior leaders together for a quick huddle. I'd say, "Okay guys, here's what we need to do. Give me some good ideas on how we can best accomplish our mission." Certainly there were times in my career in the Army when I could not do this. For example, during armed engagements when bad guys were shooting at us, I did not have time to call everyone together to get opinions. I had to make decisions and then tell my subordinates, "This is what we're going to do. Now go make those bad guys stop shooting at us!" Luckily, most of you reading this book will never have to deal with that type of situation, so there's no excuse for you not to include your subordinate leaders in the decision making process.

If you use this method of two-way communication, you'll be amazed at the outcome. You'll receive great ideas from people you never thought would give you great ideas. It's possible you'll also receive horrible ideas from people you thought would give you great ideas. Of course, you are under no obligation to use any of the ideas your subordinate leaders put forth. However, even if you don't use ideas generated from your subordinates, at least you've given them a chance to voice their opinions and have kept the lines of communication open.

"Leaders who refuse to listen will eventually be surrounded by people who have nothing to say."
-Andy Stanley

When you do listen and implement ideas that others have brought to the table, you will help ensure that your people are buying into your leadership and it will motivate your team. If you never ask for or listen to the ideas of others, you'll end up as a leader surrounded by people who have nothing to say. In my experience, I've found that an idea from one person mixed with an idea from another person added to my own ideas often produces the best plan of action.

I once had a boss and mentor named General Bantz J. Craddock. I worked for him several times during my career in the Army. I remember him saying, "A good idea is a good idea whether it comes from a private or a general, and a bad idea is a bad idea whether it comes from a private or a general."

What he was trying to tell me was that I needed to listen to the ideas of the people who worked for me. He wanted to remind me that great ideas could come from the lowest-ranking or the highest-ranking person in the organization, and many times they would come from someone I never would have expected. However, he also told me that not all ideas are great ideas and it doesn't matter if they come from the lowest-ranking or the highest-ranking person in the organization. As a leader, you will have to figure out which ideas are good, which are bad and then make decisions. If you only use your ideas, you are limiting options based on your experience alone. Collaboration in communication will often generate the best ideas and options for action.

Listening is Part of Communication

A leader understands that good listening skills are a vital part of communication. Too many leaders today either do not understand this or don't believe it. A good leader will take the time to listen.

I don't think it's a stretch to say that many people today listen just enough to figure out what they want to say instead of listening to actually hear and learn. Subordinates will quickly figure out what kind of listener you are.

I learned two valuable lessons about listening while working at the Army National Training Center where I had the honor of working for Lieutenant Colonel Joseph Fil. He taught me what it meant to really listen to people and how that part of your communication skills can be very powerful.

"The majority of people do not listen in order to understand, but instead they listen in order to reply."
-Stephen Covey

During my first year at the National Training Center my job was to help Lieutenant Colonel Fil put together After Action Reviews or AARs. His job was to give the visiting battalion commander and his junior leaders an AAR after each simulated combat mission. Lieutenant Colonel Fil would tell me what he wanted as the theme of the AAR. My job was to produce the slides that showed the points Lieutenant Colonel Fil wanted to discuss and why those points were important. It was a simple, albeit time consuming, job.

Before each AAR, Lieutenant Colonel Fil would go over each slide and rehearse his presentation. During those rehearsals, he would always have two or three of us in the room with him. Many times Lieutenant Colonel Fil would ask each of us in the room why the concept he was trying to emphasize was important. He would listen to what each of us had to say about that point. He would then address each of us telling us what was correct or incorrect in our views of each point. It was obvious to all of us that he had actually listened to us and then took the time to address each of us individually. Even though we were in a time-constrained environment, he took the time to listen to us and teach us something when he certainly didn't have to. That was a powerful lesson.

***

"There is only one rule for being a good talker – learn to listen."
-Christopher Morley

***

The second way Lieutenant Colonel Fil imparted the importance of listening to me was even simpler, but just as powerful. Most mornings as I walked into work I would pass Lieutenant Colonel Fil in the hallway. I would usually greet him with, "Good morning, sir."

Without fail, he would say, "Good morning. How are you doing?" He would not just say, "Good morning. How are you doing?" in passing. He would say it and then stop and actually listen to how I was doing. He was not satisfied with a simple answer like, "Fine." or "I'm doing well." After I explained how I was, he would ask how my wife Kelly was doing and then he'd ask how both my children, Oak and Caileigh, were doing. He truly wanted to know and actively listened to me as I answered. He was a busy man, but I never once saw him look at his watch to hint that he did not have time to listen. During our conversations, he never once acted as if he needed to be doing something more important than talking with me. If there were issues or some interesting events going on in our lives, he would ask about them. The fact that he cared enough about me to really listen to me sent a powerful message, a lesson I've never forgotten.

Handwritten Notes

One thing I've learned throughout my career as a leader is the importance of sending hand-written notes. In my opinion, a hand-written note or letter can be one of the most powerful forms of communication.

"Never underestimate the power of a hand written note or letter."
-Anonymous

A hand-written note means you not only thought about the person, but it tells them they are so important that it was worth your time to sit down and write a personal message.

It really doesn't matter why you are sending a hand-written note. It could be to thank someone for something. It could be to congratulate a person on an outstanding accomplishment. It could be as simple as letting someone know they are a valued member of the team. It really doesn't matter why you write a note or letter. In my experience, whenever I've done this, I've always gotten good results.

Communicating without Misunderstanding

When good leaders communicate with their people, they are clear, concise, succinct and easily understood. The old adage "If it can be misunderstood, it will be" is absolutely correct. Have you ever asked the people who work for you to do something and when the project was completed it was not at all what you had asked for? I know I have. I can think of several times when I asked my soldiers to complete a project. I gave them what I thought were specific instructions. They worked hard on it and when it was completed, they would report back. When I looked at the finished product, it was not what I had asked for. I would say, "This is not what I asked you to do."

"Yes, sir, it is," they'd respond.

I would go back and look at the instructions I had given them. Sure enough, they had given me exactly what I had asked for. It wasn't what I wanted, but it was what I had asked for. Good leaders will communicate directions in such a manner that everybody understands them. If they don't, they'll get exactly what they asked for.

Throughout my years as a leader, I have figured out one simple way to avoid the scenario I just described. It's not a new concept and it's certainly not something I invented, but it works.

"How well you listen determines how well you connect, and connection is key to leadership."
-John Eades

I trust that most people reading this book have heard of the Emperor Napoleon Bonaparte. Napoleon would direct battles while sitting atop his beautiful white stallion. Next to him would always stand a low ranking soldier like a corporal. As the battle raged, Napoleon often found it necessary to send out new orders to his generals. He would quickly formulate the necessary orders, but before issuing them to his generals, he would issue them to the corporal standing next to him. After issuing the orders to the corporal, he would ask the young soldier to repeat back to him, in his own words, what the orders required him to do. If the corporal understood the orders, then Napoleon would forward that order to his generals. If the corporal did not understand the orders, then Napoleon figured one of his generals could misinterpret the orders and he would start over. It was a simple and effective way to make sure his orders were clear, concise, succinct and easily understood.

As leaders, we could all use a Napoleon's corporal. Any leader could stand to have a person to bounce ideas off of before issuing directions to people in the organization. That person should be someone you trust and perhaps someone who's not afraid to hurt your feelings. It should not be a yes-man or somebody that will tell you what they think you want to hear. It should be somebody willing to give you the answers you need to hear. Throughout my career I have been lucky. My Napoleon's corporal has always been my wife. I believe she would tell you that I have been hers as well. She has always told me the truth, even when she knew it might hurt my feelings. There have been countless times when I've come home and said to her, "Guess what I'm going to do?" I would tell her my plans, she would listen and then she would tell me honestly if she thought it was a great idea. If she thought it was a horrible idea, she would tell my exactly why she thought that. She has saved me from doing a lot of dumb things over the years. Find yourself a Napoleon's corporal and, I promise you, you'll save yourself from making a lot of bad decisions.

Roger Hughes, the head football coach at Stetson University and a good friend of mine, told me that in addition to appointing captains for his football team, he also appoints two or three communication officers. He charges them with making him aware of times when the other members of the team misunderstand his vision or orders. They also know they have the right to come to his office any time and let him know they think he needs to tell the team something again due to confusion. It's a great idea and something that I've tried to incorporate into my leadership style.

Conducting Meetings

Another important way organizations communicate is through meetings. If you're like me, I'm sure you've sat through many boring and worthless meetings. If you're the leader, the responsibility for conducting productive meetings rests on your shoulders.

It's not difficult to conduct an efficient and effective meeting. There are three simple things you can do to accomplish this.

First, a good leader will have an agenda prepared before the meeting. Not only is it important to set an agenda, but it's important to hand that agenda out a few days before the meeting. The reason for this is simple. When people come to a meeting knowing what's going to be discussed, they can prepare themselves. They can do some research and contribute to the conversation. I can remember too many times when I've sat through meetings where my superiors wanted to talk about upcoming events or projects but nobody knew what was going to be discussed so nobody had a chance to prepare. If we had been given an agenda ahead of time, we could have shown up at the meeting prepared to discuss items on the agenda.

Second, a good leader sets a time limit on a meeting. My general rule of thumb is that no meeting should last longer than an hour. If I'm sitting in a meeting and it goes longer than an hour, you're going to lose me. I may still be there in person, but I'll no longer be thinking about what's being discussed. I'll be thinking about fishing, the upcoming football game, drinking a beer or something else, but it will not be what's going on in the meeting. Have a time limit and stick to it no matter what. The shorter the meeting, the better.

"As a leader, you must consistently drive effective communication. Meetings must be deliberate and intentional – your organizational rhythm should value purpose over habit and effectiveness over efficiency."
-Chris Fussel

Third, a good leader sticks to the agenda. Too many times people start talking about items or ideas that are not on the agenda. They might be great ideas or important items, but if they're not on the agenda, they should not be discussed. Again, this has happened to me many times. When I run a meeting, if somebody gets way off topic, I'll say, "That's a great idea, but it's not for this meeting. Let's discuss it in my office after the meeting or at the next meeting, but not right now." It's not always easy to do this, but it's necessary if you want to conduct effective and efficient meetings.

When you are in a position of leadership and are in charge of meetings, you can make the meetings productive or you can waste people's time. If you follow these three simple steps, I promise you people will want to come to your meetings because they know you'll have an agenda prepared in advance, you'll keep the meeting short and you'll stick to the topics at hand. Commit yourself and your organization to running effective and efficient meetings. As a leader it's the right thing to do.

Key Take-aways

- Clear and concise instructions and expectations are necessary if you want people in your organization to understand what you are asking of them.

- Good listening skills are imperative for all leaders at any level.

- It's important for leaders to run efficient and effective meetings.

Reflections

- Make a special effort to communicate in a way that is easy to understand and cannot be misunderstood.

- Make an effort to listen to and understand what someone else is saying, not just so you can give your response to what was said.

- Use the three-step process to ensure that meetings are productive and useful for your organization.

Guest speaker at Memorial Day Ceremony
DeLand, FL - 2016

With fellow veterans on Memorial Day
DeLand, FL - 2016

Notes

Chapter 5

A Leader Teaches and Trains

*"Train people well enough so they can leave;
treat them well enough so they don't want to."*
-Richard Branson

AS A LEADER in the Army, my two most important jobs
were simple: complete my missions and take care of my people.
These two concepts translate to any business or organization.
They are closely related and interdependent. If you take care of
your people, which includes teaching and training them, they will
take care of you by accomplishing the missions you assign them.

As I travel around and talk about leadership, I always tell
people that one of their top priorities as leaders will be to teach

and train the people that work for them. If you teach the people under you how to do their jobs effectively, you will have more time to do the things that only the leader can do. Remember, there are things that only the leader can do. If this wasn't the case, there would be no need for leaders at all.

"No man will make a great leader who wants to do it all himself or get all the credit for doing it."
-Andrew Carnegie

In my experience, becoming a micromanager is the number one mistake a leader can make. It's easy to understand why this can occur. First of all, if a leader is focused on accomplishing a mission, there will always be some fear of failure – fear that the chance of failure increases if subordinates are given too much freedom to do their jobs. Lack of trust that those who work for them will do their jobs correctly is one of the main reasons that leaders become micromanagers.

The second reason is that it's easy sometimes for leaders to believe that they can accomplish a job quicker than the people they assigned to the task. However, when a leader takes over the responsibilities of the workers, there is less time to do the things that only the leader can do.

Micromanaging

Have you ever had a boss that assigned you a task, only to micromanage every aspect of that task? I know I have. I've had bosses that would assign me a task and then take the execution of that task completely out of my hands. They would look over my shoulder and tell me they would not do things that way. Or they'd tell me they preferred if I did things this way. When that occurred, I would simply say, "You assigned this task to me. Let me accomplish it the way I see fit."

I understand why leaders fall into the micromanaging mode, but I can promise you they are not helping their workers when they do it, nor are they helping the organization. A good leader will resist the temptation to say, "It's easier for me to do it than to teach someone else how to do it." That will only undermine your employees, your organization and your own effectiveness as a leader.

When I give leadership presentations, I talk a lot about the dangers of micromanaging people. The truth is, every time you micromanage someone, you are cheating that person out of an experience. That person is not learning how to do something important. To take it one step further, you have not only cheated that person out of an important experience, you have cheated other people who may someday work for that person out of that experience. If you don't allow your employees to accomplish their tasks, it will be difficult for them to teach others how to do the same tasks in the future. Micromanaging your people can have a negative effect on your organization for a long time.

As a leader, it can be difficult to watch a subordinate struggle with a task they've been given. I get that. But if you want your organization to grow and get better, it's critical that you teach your people to do their jobs so that when you give them a task to perform, they can do it.

When I was an infantry lieutenant, I wanted to be the scout platoon leader. Every infantry and armor lieutenant wants that job. There is only one scout platoon in each infantry or armor battalion and that is the prized position every lieutenant works toward.

One day my battalion commander called me into his office and told me that I was going to take over the scout platoon in a couple months after the current platoon leader had departed. I was thrilled. However, things did not quite work out that way. About a month later, one of the mortar platoons in the division had an accident on the range that killed the mortar platoon leader and three soldiers. As a result of this training accident, every mortar platoon in the division came under scrutiny. My battalion commander relieved the mortar platoon leader in our battalion because of some things he was doing that had left serious safety breaches.

Eventually, my battalion commander called me back into his office and said, "Oak, I know I promised you the scout platoon, but we have a problem. The mortar platoon has some problems and I need someone to fix those problems." He said, "Tag, you're it!" He went on to say, "Oh, by the way, the division will evaluate the mortar platoon in three months." As it turned out, instead of taking charge of the scout platoon, I was put in charge of the mortar platoon.

As unhappy as I was about the decision, I was still a soldier and did as I had been instructed. I went home that evening and began to formulate a plan on how I was going to fix the mortar platoon. The first thing I knew I had to fix was how my soldiers conducted live fire exercises. It was determined after the accident that several mortar platoons were not following correct procedures while firing live ammunition. I knew everything else was secondary and I could easily fix those problems in a short amount of time, but if I didn't fix the live fire issues, soldiers might die.

I reported to my battalion commander and started to lay out my plan on how I was going to get the mortar platoon ready for the division inspection, but more importantly, how I was going to get the platoon ready to fight in the next war. He was agreeing with everything I had to say until I told him we were going to the range to fire live ammunition the following week. He told me he thought that going to the range and firing live ammunition five days after the training accident that killed four soldiers was too soon. I said, "Boss, you pay this platoon to put live mortar rounds down range. If they cannot do that safely then why do we have a mortar platoon?" He reluctantly agreed to my plan.

Monday we deployed to the range. I started with the basics and had my soldiers conduct dry fire exercises. That means they were going through the motions of firing live ammunition, but there were no live shells. I wanted to make sure they knew what they were doing before they went live. I did not want to end up like the other mortar platoon leader and those three soldiers.

***

"A boss who micromanages is like a coach who wants to get in the game. Leaders guide and support and then sit back to cheer from the sidelines."
-Simon Sinek

***

My plan was to have my soldiers conduct dry fire exercises the entire first day. Sometime during that first morning, I noticed my soldiers had stopped and were looking past me. When I turned around to see what they were looking at, I saw the battalion commander. I figured he was checking up on the new platoon leader. Given the circumstances, I could totally understand. However, on day two, while conducting the same dry fire exercises the same thing happened again. When I turned around, I saw the battalion commander observing us again.

I told my soldiers to take a break. I asked the battalion

commander to go for a walk with me. We walked into the woods, far away from my soldiers, and we had a discussion. I told him that either he was going to fix the mortar platoon or I was. I didn't care which one he chose, but we both could not fix the platoon. After a somewhat heated exchange, he realized that I was correct. I reminded him of my plan, a plan he agreed to. I assured him I would fix the problems in the platoon, but he needed to trust me and leave me alone. He finally agreed, left the range and left us alone. Three months later the mortar platoon received a perfect score on its evaluation and two months after that, when we deployed to the National Training Center, our mortar platoon set all kinds of records for the number of rounds fired both live and virtual.

The best leaders are the ones who have the sense to surround themselves with outstanding people and have the self-restraint not to meddle in how they do their jobs. Good leaders will train their people to do their jobs and then trust them to do their jobs correctly.

Trusting Your People

One thing I figured out early in my career as a leader is to never tell someone how to do things. I don't want this to sound contradictory to the first part of this chapter. Obviously, a leader has to teach and train the people under them. Over time, however, I developed my own philosophy about telling people how to do things. I realized that if I needed to tell somebody exactly how to do every task, I could just do everything myself. Telling somebody how to do something is different from giving advice. If somebody asks me for advice relative to a project, of course I will share information with them, but I will not do the task for them.

General George S. Patton, one of my heroes and one of the greatest leaders this country has ever produced, once said, "Never tell people how to do things. Tell them what you want done and they will surprise you with their ingenuity." I have always loved this quote and have tried to put it into practice. If you don't, several things can happen.

"The greatest leader is not necessarily the one who does the greatest things.
He is the one that gets the people to do the greatest things."
-Ronald Reagan

First, every person is different and is comfortable handling problems and dealing with issues in his or her own way. By forcing someone to do a task the way you would do it, you may not be getting the best out of that person. If you allow them to work through the issues and accomplish the assigned tasks on their own, they will have to use their own talents and abilities.

Second, by forcing people to do tasks the way you would do them limits the scope of ideas that could be generated by others. At that point, the organization is only taking advantage of your knowledge and your experiences, or, in some cases, the lack thereof. By allowing the people who work for you to tackle the issues of the assigned task on their own, you are allowing them to use their experiences, their knowledge and their talents. I don't care how long you've been doing your job or how long you've been a leader, you don't have a corner on all the ways to accomplish a given task. I have discovered there are always multiple ways to get things done, even if the way someone else chooses is a way you would never have gone. The infusion of other people's ideas, experiences and talents, added to your own, will only make your people and your organization stronger.

Third, if you always tell your people how to accomplish tasks, they will become overly dependent on you. An overly dependent worker will often become a lazy worker. A good leader will allow people to make decisions and do their jobs without becoming overly dependent.

When I assign tasks to my employees, I use what I call objectives and guideposts. I'll tell the person to whom I've assigned a task what I expect the outcome of the project will look like – the objective. Then I'll provide reasonable limits from left to right, so to speak – the guideposts. For example, I'll tell the person how much money they have to budget, other resources they'll have at their disposal, which people on the team will be available to help them and how much time they have to complete the project. Then I get out of the way and let the person do the job that was assigned.

In my experience over the years, I've discovered that this is almost always enough for people to run with and to accomplish the task at hand. This doesn't mean I don't check on their progress, because I do. I schedule in-progress reviews every week or so. It also doesn't mean I wash my hands of the project. If they have questions they can certainly come ask me and I'm happy to help. However, I let them accomplish the tasks the way they see fit. If you use this method, your people will come up with results that will absolutely surprise you. They may not do the project the way you would have done it, but they will accomplish what you asked. In the end, it doesn't always matter how they reached the objective as long as they gave you what you asked for and stayed within your guideposts.

"Trust is the foundation of leadership."
-John C. Maxwell

I will tell you, using this method requires you to have faith in your people. That is a good thing. Knowing you have faith in them will energize them. They will work extra hard to give you what you have asked for because they know you have faith in them and you are counting on them. It also requires you to give up some of your control over the situation. General Craddock once told me, "The most difficult part of leadership is letting go, trusting in subordinate leaders and allowing them the freedom to do their jobs." However, if you have the courage to do so, you will be pleasantly surprised by what your people can and will do. I would encourage you to try this method next time you assign a task to an employee. I'm confident you will like the results.

Delegating

As I give my leadership presentations, I'm often asked why delegating is included in the *Train Your Subordinates* section of my presentation. I explain to them that developing subordinate leaders is a huge part of the training they will be responsible for as leaders. It's always been my belief that true leaders do not create followers; true leaders create more leaders.

"The best of all leaders is the one that develops their people so that eventually they don't need them anymore."
-Lao Tzu

As a leader, you cannot be everywhere. I'd like to think sometimes that I'm Superman, but even I have not figured out how to be in two places at the same time. Along those same lines, you cannot do everything yourself. In fact, if you're trying to do everything yourself, you are hurting your employees and your organization.

Good leaders learn to delegate as many things as possible to their junior leaders. That is a huge part of being a leader. It's not always easy to delegate, but it's necessary for an organization and its people to reach their full potential.

Even though I always encourage other leaders to learn to delegate, I'm always quick to remind people that you can delegate authority but you can never delegate responsibility. As the leader, responsibility is yours and yours alone. The leader will be the one blamed when things go wrong. Jocko Willink, a retired Navy SEAL and motivational speaker, once said, "As a leader you must own everything in your world. There is no one else to blame."

John C. Maxwell, an American author, speaker and pastor, said, "Leaders become great, not because of their power, but because of their ability to empower others." I believe this with my whole heart. A good leader will establish boundaries for what team members are allowed to do, but for them to truly rise to their full potential, they need to know what authority they have.

Train your employees to do their jobs. Give them tasks with minimal guidance and let them do the jobs you trained them to do. Empower those who work for you and you will be amazed at what they can do for your organization.

Mentoring

A good leader can also be a valuable mentor. If you believe, as I do, that your job as a leader is to teach the next generation of leaders, then you will also be willing to mentor others. Mentoring is not necessarily the same as leading. Mentoring is more focused on you passing on knowledge to somebody who will someday replace you.

"While I made my living as a coach, I have lived my life to be a mentor and to be mentored. Everything in this world has been passed down. Every piece of knowledge is something that has been shared by someone else. If you understand it as I do, mentoring becomes your true legacy. It is the greatest inheritance you can give to others. It is why you get up every day, to teach and be taught."
-John Wooden

If you take leadership seriously, you will happily be willing to mentor members of the next generation. In my recent experience, I've noticed that Millennials seem to have less experience forming relationships with mentors from an older generation.

I've been lucky in my career. I've had several bosses, some of whom became two, three or four-star generals in the Army, that for whatever reasons decided they would like to mentor me. Being connected and having access to these mentors throughout my career was invaluable. Sometimes that mentorship involved them reaching out to me in order to teach me something, while other times it was me reaching out to them to gather their opinions or to ask them questions. I was granted access to successful, powerful people who were willing to help guide me down my career path and influence my leadership style. I know for a fact that having access to these mentors helped me immeasurably in my career as a leader.

Following is one example of how having access to these mentors was helpful to me: as an officer in the Army, you generally move duty positions (get a new job) every year and duty locations at least every two years. Every couple of years my assignment officer would call and tell me what positions were available to me. I would immediately call General Craddock and say, "Hey boss, branch is offering these positions." Without fail, for every position offered, he would give me one of two answers. If branch offered me a position and location that General Craddock thought was good he would tell me to take it. If branch was offering me a position he thought was not a good fit for me, he would say, "Run, Oak, run very fast." This simple advice was invaluable to me. I would call my assignment officer back and tell him which position I was willing to accept.

As important as I believe it is to be willing to mentor others, I would also emphasize that you can't be a mentor to everyone. There simply isn't enough time. The advice I give leaders is to choose those one or two in your organization that are diamonds in the rough – those who you believe have the capacity and abilities to be future leaders in the organization. Let them know you would like to mentor them. Make yourself available to them. Then, live up that promise

I tell every young man and woman I commission as a second lieutenant that if they ever need anything they should feel free to contact me. I still have young men and women that I commissioned as far back as 2006 who have stayed in contact with me. They don't all come to me for advice or help. Many just keep me updated on their careers. However, I do have a handful who have come to me regularly to seek my advice, and I'm always happy to help.

At some point you will no longer be a leader in your organization. Either you will move on to a bigger and better position in another organization or you will retire. Good leaders will make sure they train new leaders who will replace them and eventually run the organization. Take that obligation seriously. The future of your organization depends on it.

Providing Feedback

Good leaders provide feedback to their people. Face-to-face counseling between leaders and their people can be very effective. One aspect of a leader's responsibility is to talk to people in the organization to let them know how they're doing. It's critical to give both positive and negative constructive feedback.

Most people enjoy receiving feedback after doing a job well. A pat on the back is always appreciated. It's important for leaders to let people know when they are doing great work. Napoleon Bonaparte understood the importance of positive feedback and rewarding people for their efforts. He once said, "Give me enough ribbon, and I'll conquer the world!" He understood that positive reinforcement would keep his soldiers motivated. If you show the people in your organization appreciation, they will want to work hard for you.

"We all need people who will give us feedback. That's how we improve."
-Bill Gates

As important as it is to give your people positive feedback for a job well done, it's just as important to let them know when they are not meeting the standards of the organization. Many times during my career, I've had to call people into my office and tell them they were not working up to the standards that were expected of them. Surprisingly, many of them were shocked to hear those words from me. They had no idea they were not meeting the standards expected of them.

If you have somebody who is not working up to your organization's standards and you haven't taken the time to have a face-to-face meeting with that person, his or her failure will be partly your fault. It's possible that person may not know or understand your expectations. The only way for them to know that you are not happy with their performance is if you tell them.

It's not enough just to tell somebody he or she is not meeting standards; a good leader will explain ways to fix the problem. Then it will be up to that person to make changes and meet the standards expected in the organization. They will also have to be ready to accept the consequences if they don't make changes.

As an officer in the United States Army, I was required to conduct face-to-face counseling sessions with all the people that worked for me once a quarter. It was a time-consuming, yet important, process. This allowed me to tell the people who worked for me that either they were meeting the standards expected of them or they weren't. By doing this on a regular basis, nobody in the organization would go more than three months without receiving feedback on their performance. These quarterly evaluations gave them the insight they needed to make changes, if necessary, to meet the standards expected of them or to keep doing what they were doing. This process worked for the Army, and I promise it can work for you, no matter what profession you're in or how many people you lead.

My son, Oakland Vincent McCulloch, graduated from the United States Military Academy at West Point. He spent his time as an officer in the Army and then decided to use his skills in the business world. The largest construction company in the world, a multi-national company, hired him as a management trainee. The part of the company he was positioned in is an aggregate distribution terminal served primarily by rail. They bring in rock and sand from their own mining operations before selling and distributing that material to asphalt, construction and landscaping companies.

He was a management trainee for 18 months. During that time, he learned how and where all the jobs were done, many of which included manual labor. After that initial period of training, the company promoted him to a position called Lead Rail, where he was in charge of four people. He quickly learned that no one on his team, including him, had received any face-to-face counseling until it was time for an annual appraisal. After a short time, my son was promoted to a position called Area Manager. In that position, he ran three rail terminals and was in charge of 10 people. When he assumed the position of Area Manager, he implemented a quarterly counseling session for each of his employees like the ones he had been part of in the Army. Every member of his team met with him every three months. This was a completely new concept for his organization.

Shortly after, the company added two more terminals to his charge. That made a total of four terminals and 24 employees, five of whom were in the role of Lead Rail. At that point, he realized he needed to delegate some of the authority and workload for the quarterly counseling to his Lead Rails. Senior leaders cannot counsel everyone they are in charge of due to time constraints. They must delegate and trust subordinate leaders to do some of the work. So now, once a quarter, he counsels his Lead Rails and his Lead Rails counsel their employees at each terminal.

Because his employees are receiving regular feedback on their performance, both good and bad, they now know not only what he expects of them, but also whether or not they are meeting those expectations. This has allowed my son to increase the performance and production of his team. He has also provided focus and direction for each member of his team, including the main area where each member needs to focus his or her efforts.

Oak explains, "If you could plot your team's success on a map, then quarterly performance reviews would be your azimuth checks." He has proven that face-to-face counseling works, whether it's in the Army or in a civilian company. If you are not conducting face-to-face counseling on a regular basis in your organization, try implementing this strategy. You will see what a tremendous difference it makes.

Key Take-aways

- Good leaders allow for autonomy and provide generous feedback to the people in their organizations.

- Good leaders delegate authority to their subordinate leaders to enhance their abilities to accomplish jobs.

- Good leaders avoid micromanaging.

- Good leaders allow their teams to solve problems creatively, thereby building their investment in the mission.

Reflections

- Take some time to think about how to best teach and train the people who work for you. Good leaders won't micromanage but will empower their people to make important decisions.

- If you are not providing feedback to the members of your team on a regular basis, figure out a way to do it. You will like the results.

- Next time you assign a task to a team member, try using the objectives and guideposts method described in this chapter.

Veteran's Day with Commander James Patterson
Port Orange, FL – 2015

Commissioning Ceremony, Stetson University - 2014

Notes

Chapter 6

A Leader Solves Problems

"Great leaders are almost always great simplifiers who can cut through arguments, debates and doubt, to offer a solution everybody can understand."
-Colin Powell

GOOD LEADERS ARE almost always great problem solvers. They are able to identify problems, come up with solutions to solve those problems and implement and supervise the plans to effectively make necessary changes. That does not only include problems in the day-to-day operations of an organization, but it also includes the problems of individuals within the organization.

Solving Problems in Your Organization

If you want to solve any problem in your organization, the first thing you have to learn is to be brutally honest – honest with yourself, your boss and the people who work for you. It's difficult for a leader to solve problems without being honest about those problems. It's not always easy, but it's absolutely necessary.

"One of the true tests of leadership is the ability to recognize a problem before it becomes an emergency."
-Arnold Glasgow

When President Eisenhower, the great U.S. Army general, encountered a problem in his organization, the first thing he would do is search for the source of that problem. He would get up and walk a circle around his desk. If he didn't find the source there he would walk a bigger circle around the offices near his. If he still didn't find the source of the problem, he would walk a larger circle. He would keep expanding the circle until he found the source of the problem.

Why did he start by walking a circle around his own desk? He started there because he knew that he may have been the source of the problem. That sort of self-awareness is critical. It's not uncommon for leaders themselves to be the source of problems in an organization. Bad ideas are a dime a dozen, and maybe some leaders don't have a Napoleon's corporal with whom they can share ideas. I can't tell you how many times I've cringed when a boss of mine would put out something he had decided to do that to me seemed ill-conceived. In the back of my mind I'd think, "When I'm in charge, I will never do that."

I catalogued experiences like that and drew on those experiences later, when I actually was in charge.

"The true test of leadership is how well you function in a crisis."
-Brian Tracy

A good leader is not afraid to confront the source of a problem in an organization. The difficulty lies in the fact that it's sometimes people in an organization above the leader that are the cause of the problem. Confronting a superior is never easy and may not always be the best thing for your career, but sometimes it's necessary to get to the root of a problem and take steps to solve it.

What if it's an employee who is the cause of a problem? That can be just as tricky as when it's a superior. You don't want to upset the person, especially if he or she is one of your best employees. You need to be honest with them, but you must figure out a way to confront them that makes the situation better, not worse. Finally, if you are the problem, you'll have to put your pride and ego aside and fix yourself. That is seldom easy to do, but it's absolutely necessary if you really want to solve a problem. Again, honesty is the key.

Once you have figured out what the problem is and have found the source of the problem, then you have to figure out a solution to fix the problem. There may be one way or several ways to fix the problem. My advice is that once you have identified the problem, figure out who in your organization is the expert in the area you are trying to fix and consult that person. After all, who knows better than somebody who does that task every day?

When I was growing up, my father's best friend worked at the Chrysler assembly plant in the next town over. He had worked in the same department of that plant for 38 years. He spent most of those years installing fenders and bumpers on whatever vehicles the plant produced. If the people in charge of that plant had a problem with fenders or bumpers, who do you think they would talk to? Of course! They would talk to my father's friend who had 38 years of experience in that area. He most likely knew there was a problem even before his bosses did.

A good leader will know who the experts are in an organization and use them to help identify and solve problems when they arise. Once a problem has been identified, a good leader will develop a plan of action to fix that problem. I've found that it's helpful to pull in subordinates, the ones who will be implementing the solution, to help plan the solution.

I've always tried to involve as many junior leaders as possible when tackling a problem. In some cases, I've asked everybody in the organization to help develop a plan to solve a problem. I'll gather my junior leaders together, explain the problem to them and ask them for their ideas and advice.

What usually happens is this: I will take an idea or something from several different people, add in a few things of my own and put it all together in a plan designed to solve the problem. This fosters a feeling of ownership for those who are going to implement the plan to fix the problem. By doing this, it's no longer just the boss's plan; it's everybody's plan to fix the problem. By tapping into the experience and expertise of others, a good leader will expand his or her own experience and expertise.

Once you've identified the problem, develop and implement a plan to solve the problem. Then, hold your people accountable for following through if you actually want to fix the problem. A good leader gives people a timeframe in which to accomplish assigned tasks. Along with a timeframe are quality standards that will be met along the way. People appreciate a timeframe and will perform better if they know there are high expectations for their work.

The last, and often most important, part of the problem-solving strategy is for you, the leader, to follow up. If you do not follow up to make sure the changes you implemented are actually occurring, then you will have wasted your time and the time of your organization. If you don't follow up, your employees will go right back to doing things the way they were always done. Why? Human beings are creatures of habit. I talk about this in my leadership presentations. I ask people to think about some of the things they do every day: how they put on their shoes, how they shave, etc. People tend to do the same things exactly the same way every day.

When I worked at Stetson University, I walked to work every day since I only lived three blocks from my office. There were five or six different routes I could have taken. How many of those routes did I use? That's right. I walked to work the same way every day. It wasn't because I put a lot of thought into it. In fact, I didn't think about it at all, I just did it out of habit. On the rare occasions when I drove, I usually arrived at work early, before everyone else. That allowed me to park in my favorite spot right outside my office door. Once in a while, somebody else would arrive at work before me and take my parking spot and I would have to park somewhere else. On those days, when I left the office in the evening, where do you think I'd walk? Of course, I'd walk to my favorite spot even though I hadn't parked there. I did it out of habit without thinking.

If you fail to follow up with your employees to monitor the plans you implemented to fix a problem, more than likely your people will go back to doing things the way they had done them before, purely out of habit.

"Change is not popular; we are creatures of habit as human beings. I want it to be the way it was, but if you continue the way it was, there will be no new way it is."
-Robin Williams

When I cut the grass at home, I start in the same location and cut exactly the same way, almost step by step, every time. One day I went out to cut the grass, and when I got to my starting spot my wife was working in the yard. When I told her I would have to wait until she was finished for me to start she said, "Why?"

I said, "You're in my starting spot."

She started laughing and said, "Why can't you start in a different spot?"

I did start somewhere else, as hard as it was, but I was messed up the entire time. We are creatures of habit.

When I took over as the associate director of the food bank, I was in charge of day-to-day operations. A large part of that job was organizing food pickups from the sources that donated to us and then delivering that food to organizations that distributed it to people in their communities. We dispatched many trucks every day. Our drivers each had their own pickup and delivery routes. In theory, that sounds simple, but in reality it was rather complicated.

First, due to vacation time, sick time and other schedule glitches, the same drivers didn't always cover the same routes every day. Second, depending on the day of the week or month, the routes were not exactly the same. Third, each organization we worked with had different hours of operation. Finally, there were always changes or opportunities that became available after the trucks had departed on their routes.

With all these variables to deal with, developing a daily schedule for each truck was a nightmare. Even after I had the route schedules set up, I was never sure the routes we developed were the most efficient in the use of time and money. This was the first big problem I needed to fix, and I knew I would need some help.

I called our parent organization, Feeding America, and told them about my issue. I figured I was not the only one dealing with this problem, and I was right. As a result, Feeding America reached out to FedEx, which has one of the largest truck fleets in America, and got them to offer the food banks the software they use for their routes. They also got FedEx to agree to train people from each food bank in the organization that wished to use this system. Our food bank was one of the five selected to be in the pilot program.

Once we had this program up and running we could easily develop the daily routes for each of our trucks. In addition, we were able to determine which routes were most efficient, both in terms of time and money. We also were able to track each truck's location in real time so we could take advantage of any opportunities that became available throughout the day along those routes. We still listened to the drivers' feedback to make sure things were set up correctly, to make sure everything ran smoothly and the routes made sense. Implementing this program at the food bank to fix the truck-routing problem was just one of the many reasons I was able to help increase the amount of food we distributed annually from 1.4 million pounds to 3.2 million pounds in the 18 months I was there.

Helping Employees Fix Their Problems

Throughout this book, I've tried to emphasize that leadership is not all about you. It's about serving your organization and serving other people. In addition to being a problem solver for an organization, good leaders will also help the people working for them solve their own problems.

Of course you won't have every answer for every problem brought to you by those who work for you. In those cases, a good leader will find somebody else in the organization or somebody outside the organization than can help in some way. That has happened many times throughout my career as a leader.

Following are two such examples: When I was the commander for a basic training company, I would receive a new group of soldiers every few months. Many of them came with existing personal problems. For some, the problems they had were the reason they joined the Army in the first place.

Soon after I took over as the company commander one of my privates asked to set up an appointment to speak with me about a problem. When he came into my office, I asked him to sit down. I started by trying to make sure he felt comfortable speaking with me. I knew it could be intimidating for a private to be speaking with his company commander (a captain), so I wanted to put him as much at ease as I could. I asked him how basic training was going and what his favorite and least favorite parts were thus far. After that, I asked him to tell me about his problem. He told me that before he enlisted in the Army he had gotten his girlfriend pregnant. I told him that I could certainly help him figure out how to handle that situation. My soldier quickly let me know that that was not the only problem. I said, "Oh? What's the rest of the problem?"

He said, "I also got her mom pregnant."

I said "Son, there's nothing I can do to help you with that problem." However, I did set up an appointment for him to visit the unit chaplain. I figured the chaplain was better equipped to handle the emotional needs of the private than I was. In the end, I didn't just pass him off to the chaplain and forget about him. A couple weeks later, I made sure I found this soldier during a break in training and asked him how he was doing. I wanted him to know that I cared and that I was still available for him if he needed to speak with me again.

There have been many times in my career when I was able to help my employees through problems they were having. When I was an infantry platoon leader as a young second lieutenant at Fort Stewart, Georgia, I had a young soldier come up to me and tell me he was having money issues. After doing a little digging into his case, I figured out I could actually help him solve his problem. This young man was just spending and wasting his money on silly things and was not trying to save anything. At the time, he was over $5,000 in debt. I told him I could help him, but he would have to agree to do exactly what I told him to do. I told him he could not spend a single penny that I didn't approve and if he did, I would no longer be available to help him. He agreed to this and started to follow my directions. I developed a budget for him that paid his mandatory bills first. The second thing the budget did was allow for a certain amount to be paid on his debt. Finally, I allowed him a minimal amount of spending money each month. To his credit, he followed the budget carefully. A couple times he came and asked for more money to spend on silly things and I told him no. By the time I left my position as the platoon leader, the young man was not only out of debt, he was actually saving money.

Good leaders are great problem solvers, not just for the organization as a whole, but also for the people that work there. Honesty is the key – honesty with yourself, your boss and the people who work for you.

Key Take-aways

- Good leaders will help solve problems for the organization and its individual team members.

- Good leaders strive to get input from key players and subject matter experts in their organizations in order to solve problems.

- Good leaders will be brutally honest with themselves, their bosses and their team members.

- Good leaders plan follow-up to ensure steps have been taken to solve problems.

Reflections

- Are you willing to look at yourself as the possible root of a problem before looking elsewhere?

- Are you willing to get ideas and input from key leaders or experts in your organization to help solve problems?

- Is there a problem in your organization right now that might be your responsibility to solve?

With LTC Todd Mitchell at Commissioning Ceremony
Stetson University - 2017

With Dr. Wendy Libby, President of Stetson University
Commissioning Ceremony - 2016

Notes

Chapter 7

A Leader Builds Effective Teams

"A team is not a group of people who work together. A team is a group of people who trust each other."
-Vince Lombardi

GOOD LEADERS UNDERSTAND team building. Putting together effective teams is one of the most important jobs a leader can have. Coach Lombardi said it well. He emphasized that putting a team together doesn't just mean assembling a group of people. He understood that those people had to learn to trust each other or there would be no team.

A huge part of building a cohesive team is fostering a culture that allows everyone to feel like he or she is part of that team. They must buy into the organization and the culture you have built. You can't accomplish this without building trust, not just between you and your employees, but also among your employees as well. Your employees must trust that you will have their best interests at heart and do what is right for them and the organization, while also trusting that their fellow workers are going to do their jobs to help accomplish the organization's goals.

"Good teams become great ones when the members trust each other enough to surrender the ME for the WE."
-Phil Jackson

Building a Winning Culture

There are many different ways to define and build a culture of trust in an organization. One of the ways the Army did this was through what they call Army values. Army values are a set of the following seven ideas that are drilled into the minds of everybody who joins: Loyalty, Duty, Respect, Selfless Service, Honor, Integrity, and Personal Courage. To help soldiers remember these seven values, the Army developed the acronym LDRSHIP. Every soldier and officer is expected to know these seven values and what they mean. These values clarify expectations and foster teamwork and camaraderie. The Army expects every soldier to live by these seven values every day. It's a constant reminder that each soldier is a valuable member of the team.

My current boss, the Professor of Military Science of the Eagle Battalion at Embry-Riddle, developed another tool to help build the culture he wanted in his organization for both the cadre and the cadets. Since the school and Army ROTC mascot is an eagle, he took the word EAGLES and made each letter represent a standard he wanted the people in the organization to live by. In this case, EAGLES stands for Empowered, Accountable, Grounded, Lethal, Engaged and Steadfast. He uses this all the time in meetings and speeches, with both the cadre and cadets, to make sure everybody understands his expectations.

Attitude is Just as Important as Talent

Good leaders surround themselves with talented people. Top leaders in every profession, in order to build strong and effective teams, will gather together the best of the best. This does not just refer to talent alone. It also refers to attitude. Most of you reading this book have probably worked with people with bad attitudes. Disgruntled people with toxic attitudes are the result of many different things. They are unhappy with the jobs they have. They are unhappy with their bosses. They are unhappy in their personal lives. Whatever the reason, workers with bad attitudes can cause a toxic decay in any organization.

A good leader will try hard to be cognizant of all the employees' attitudes. One bad attitude can be very corrosive. My daughter, Caileigh Nicholson, shared an experience with me about a co-worker who had a terrible attitude. This person's attituded ended up affecting the entire organization for which she worked.

"Surround yourself with positive people who are going to push you toward greatness."
-George Villiers

After she graduated from college, Caileigh started working for a small organization. Although there were a number of employees, she only had direct interaction with one other person on a daily basis. As you can imagine, it would be difficult not to form a relationship with someone who worked next to you for 55 hours a week.

When they first started at that job, they were both happy and grateful to be working there. Over time, her fellow employee became extremely bitter, and her attitude became toxic. As months went by, her attitude failed to improve, and my daughter began to feel the negative effects of her co-worker's increasingly bitter attitude. My daughter told me that being around the constant negative environment was exhausting and that she had started to dread going to work. Trying to stay positive while surrounded by such negativity was excruciating. She told me the enthusiasm she felt when she started the job had started to wane.

"Nothing will kill a great employee faster than watching you tolerate a bad one."
-Perry Belcher

This particular job did not require the leader of her team to be in the workspace on a regular basis. Unfortunately, that meant her boss had no idea this toxic attitude was infiltrating the team. Around the one-year mark, my daughter decided it was time to let her boss know what was happening. She could see that the team was not as pleasant or efficient as it had once been. She decided she could not spend another year working around this co-worker, yet she continued to do her job to the best of her ability. She told me some of their clients were feeling the effects as well, and their confidence in the team was dwindling.

Eventually Caileigh had a long discussion with her boss where she laid out the issues at hand. After that discussion, her boss realized it was in her best interest to remove this toxic presence from the team. Ultimately, my daughter's coworker was let go. According to my daughter, there was an immediate rise in positivity and morale in their small part of the organization.

My daughter said when she sat down with her boss she learned a few valuable lessons. First, a leader cannot fix what they don't know is broken. Second, and most importantly, a leader has to make it a priority to recognize when something in the organization is not up to certain standards.

As a leader, it's important that you take it upon yourself to find and fix what is broken. Speak to every employee individually; speak to their coworkers; speak to the people who interact with these employees on a regular basis. It's critical that you get to know your team. If this is done correctly, you will find out quickly if there is an employee with a bad attitude bringing down the morale of the team.

"You don't hire for skills, you hire for attitude. You can always teach skills."
-Simon Sinek

Once someone with a toxic attitude is identified, that person should be eliminated from the organization as quickly as possible. If done quickly and correctly, a leader can minimize the damage done and salvage the spirits of the positive employees. A good leader does not allow a bad attitude to corrupt an organization or the minds of the employees on the team. My daughter hit the nail on the head when she said, "Show me a person who has developed a poor attitude, and I will show you a person destined to climb no higher."

Putting Your Goals in Writing

Each time I have held a leadership position, I've published a document called *Leadership Philosophy* for the organization. Over the years, I've published this document many times. Many of the principles were the same no matter which organization I led. However, at times I had to modify my philosophy to fit the uniqueness of the organization. I would encourage you to develop your own leadership philosophy. It's one more way you can explain to the people in your organization what is expected of them as members of the team as well as what type of culture they can expect in the organization.

Spending Time with Your People

Good leaders can build a culture of teamwork and esprit de corps by spending time with their people. Show them they are important. Show them that what they do is valuable and meaningful. Let them know that how they feel matters to you. When I was the commander of a basic training company, I would make sure that wherever my soldiers were, I was there with them. I didn't care if it was stifling hot, freezing cold or raining. I believed it was my duty to be there with them.

One day we were on the tank range where the privates were shooting gunnery on the M1A1 main battle tank. I climbed up on top of one of our tanks and had lunch with the four privates who were operating the vehicle. They were not eating a fancy lunch. They were eating an MRE (Meal Ready to Eat), the Army's meal in a brown plastic bag. I climbed up on the tank and ate the same thing they were eating. While we were eating our delicious MREs, we started talking. I asked them questions and I allowed them to ask me questions. We talked about their goals, not just in the Army, but also in their lives after their current enlistments had ended.

"You never know when a moment and a few sincere words can have an impact on a life."
-Zig Ziglar

This specific MRE lunch on top of a tank took place in the summer of 1993. In the intervening years, I had forgotten the names of those four men. However, at least one of them remembered me. In 2019, one of those privates gave me a call when he saw that Cadet Command had selected me as Recruiter of the Year. He still remembered me after all those years. He told me that because of that conversation on a summer afternoon, he had decided to leave the Army after his enlistment, attend college, join an Army ROTC program and become an officer.

He retired from the Army after 20 years of service, started his own business and is now a very successful business leader. The reason he remembered me after all those years is because I took the time to make him feel like he was an important and valued member of the team. In the end, he recommended a young man who worked for him as a prospect for our Army ROTC program. He said he wanted this young man to come to our program because of the way I had treated him 26 years ago when I was a captain and he was a private.

Giving Credit Where Credit is Due

A leader will give credit where credit is due. It's not unusual for some people in positions of authority to take credit away from their employees after a project has been successfully completed. It's happened to me; I suspect it's happened to you. Did that make you want to work harder for that boss? Did that help foster a feeling of trust? Of course not. It probably caused you to lose confidence in that leader and made you doubt your own value.

"There is no limit to the good you can do if you don't care who gets the credit."
-George C. Marshall

My philosophy is very simple when it comes to giving credit for something a team of mine has accomplished. If my team accomplished its goals, I would go to the boss and say, "Hey boss, I'd like you to see what my team accomplished." In addition, if an individual or group of people on my team really stood out while working on this task, I would make sure to mention them by name.

If, for whatever reason, my team did not accomplish the objective, I would go to the boss and say, "Hey boss, I screwed up. We did not accomplish our task, but here's how we're going to fix it." I would take the blame for that failure, because no matter who or what caused the failure, it was my fault. As the leader, I was responsible for everything that happened with my team. If you adopt a philosophy like this, I promise you it will go a long way toward developing trust and camaraderie in your organization.

Taking Care of the People on Your Team

Good leaders understand that their main job is to take care of the organizations they lead and the people on their teams. It's always been clear to me that if I take care of the people on my team, they will help me take care of the organization.

One way to hamper the building of a strong team is by putting your career before your employees' careers. I remember plenty of times when I had a colleague say to me something like this, "I had to put off sending so-and-so to the school he needs because we have an inspection coming up and I need him here."

I always thought to myself, "What are you thinking?" Holding people back to further your own agenda will only destroy trust and make it more difficult to build an effective team.

"Leaders must always put their people before themselves. If you do that, your business will take care of itself."
-Sam Walton

Don't hold your employees back. If people need some extra education or some new type of training to further their careers, don't prevent them from getting what they need to advance. If you are willing to put your employees' interests ahead of your own, your people will go to the wall for you. They will understand and believe that they are important to the team. The old adage that "there is no I in team" is absolutely true and should be a driving force in how you treat the people you are responsible for leading.

Allowing People to Learn from Their Mistakes

Leaders allow their people to learn from mistakes. If you want the people who work for you to grow, you will allow them to learn from their mistakes. If you or your organization have a 'zero defects' mentality, you will stifle progress and growth in your employees. Many people will just sit back and wait for you to tell them exactly what to do so they won't be held accountable if it doesn't work. This is an ineffective way to run an organization. Don't get me wrong, there's a big difference between making an honest mistake and making a conscious decision to do something wrong. A good leader will make that distinction clear and let people in the organization know what's permissible and what's unacceptable.

People are going to make mistakes. I can guarantee that. There are no perfect people in this world. We all make mistakes. Making mistakes and learning from those mistakes is part of how we learn to grow as people and as organizations.

"A leader takes people where they would never go on their own."
-Hans Finzel

General Craddock once told me, "Oak, if you didn't make a mistake today, then you probably didn't do anything." Like me, he understood that everybody makes mistakes. What's important is how you respond. Do you sweep it under the rug? Do you blame somebody else? Or do you come to me and say, "Boss, I made a mistake, and here's what I'm going to do to fix it."

In that case I would say, "Good, let's fix it!"

If you adopt and exercise this attitude toward mistakes, the people who work for you will feel confident that they can take chances and if they make a mistake, it will not be a career or job-ending event. That is how you build a team. That is how you allow the people in your organization to learn and grow. If you don't adopt this attitude toward mistakes, you will stifle creativity, progress and growth of the people in your organization and the organization itself.

Motivating Your People

Good leaders are great motivators. It's the responsibility of any leader to motivate the people in the organization.

So, what's the best way to motivate the people in your organization? In my experience I can tell you that it was not just by the use of rewards and punishments. The use of rewards and punishment is a good way to train dogs, but there are other things that come into playing when trying to motivate people. I'm not saying that a leader should never use rewards or punishments. Those two things are often necessary to help maintain order and discipline. However, if those are the only two techniques you use, it's more than likely that at some point you will run out of both rewards and punishments. Then what?

As a leader, you will have to figure out what motivates your people. It won't always be money, status or power. From my experience as a leader in many different organizations, one of the most powerful motivators is giving your people a true sense of purpose. To start, you will have to identify something about your organization that is unique, and that's not always easy to do.

When I was an infantry or armor officer in the Army, that was easy. After receiving a mission I would walk into a room full of soldiers and say, "We are soldiers in the greatest army in the world! We support and defend the American way of life! We support and defend the Constitution of the United States, and we protect the people in this great country from our enemies. Let's go!" I never had a problem getting soldiers motivated with that speech. However, when I took over as the associate director of the food bank, that speech did not work. Go figure.

I actually struggled to determine what would motivate the people who worked for me at the food bank. Then I figured it out. One day I was conducting a planning meeting with my key people about one of our largest food handouts of the year. This event was going to take place in about three weeks. Things were going well and then, all of a sudden, I noticed people closing their notebooks, collecting their things and starting to stand up as if they were planning on leaving. I asked them what they were doing. They told me, almost in unison, "It's 4 o'clock. It's time to go home."

"But we're not finished with the planning meeting yet," I said

They repeated, "It's 4 o'clock, so it's time to go home."

Finally I said, "If you want to leave, then leave. However, before you go, let me remind you of something very important. In three weeks, when we conduct this food handout and a 19-year old mother has to go home without any food to feed her 2-

year old daughter because we didn't get this right, you'll be the ones to blame."

How many people do you think left the meeting? That's right. Zero. They all sat down and we finished the planning session. From that short exchange, I had put my finger on what motivated those people. They really cared about the communities they were serving and wanted to make sure we helped as many people as we could.

---

*"A man always has two reasons
for doing anything: a good reason
and the real reason."*
-J.P. Morgan

Perhaps I should have been able to figure that out before, but it took that conversation for me to understand the one thing that motivated my people above all else. They felt a strong sense of purpose working for the food bank. Helping those less fortunate in their communities was one of the reasons they worked at the food bank in the first place.

Discovering what motivates your people may not always come easily, but eventually it will become clear. My job as the leader of the food bank became much easier when I figured out that this strong sense of purpose was highly motivating to my people.

Few things a leader does are more important than building a cohesive team. It's not always easy but should be a top priority for any leader. Once you've built a team based on trust and discovered what truly motivates your people, they will do almost anything you ask of them because they know you have their best interests at heart.

Key Take-aways

- Good leaders motivate their teams by making them feel valued.

- People want to be a part of something bigger than themselves and feel a shared sense of purpose.

- Listen to people in your organization. Even if you don't use their ideas, they want to be heard.

- Give your team members opportunities to grow, both in success and in failure.

- Average leaders raise the bar on themselves; good leaders raise the bar for others; great leaders inspire others to raise their own bar.

Reflections

- The next time your team successfully finishes a project, make sure you give credit to those on your team who helped the team succeed.

- The next time your team is not successful, make sure everyone knows you accept the blame for the results, and then make sure everyone knows what the plan is to fix the situation.

- Are you taking the time and making the effort to make sure your team knows you care about them?

- Are you making sure everyone knows their role in your vision and how valuable they are in completing the mission?

- Is there someone on your team right now who would be a good candidate for a developmental opportunity? Stop waiting, and make it happen as soon as possible.

Speaking at Commissioning Ceremony
Stetson University - 2016

Notes

Chapter 8

A Leader Achieves Results

"However beautiful the strategy, you should occasionally look at the results."
-Winston Churchill

WE'VE EXPLORED SOME important ideas about leadership so far and examined characteristics that define what a good leader looks like. Things like serving others selflessly, taking charge, communicating effectively, teaching and training others, solving problems and building solid teams.

All of these things are very important. However, it's possible for a leader to do all of these things and still not be successful. There's a saying in the Army: "Mission first, people always."

That means you always take care of your people, but in the end, accomplishing the mission is the most important thing. In the end, none of those other things matter if you do not get the results you need. Results matter.

———————

*"Perfection is not attainable, but
if we chase perfection we
can catch excellence."*
-Vince Lombardi

———————

It's in vogue today for people to talk about how failure is not only okay but that it's expected, and, worse yet, that it's acceptable. That you learn more from failure than from success. You can actually see things like this on the websites of self-proclaimed leadership experts. I don't know about you, but it seems odd to me that an organization would hire somebody to tell their people that it's okay to fail. I want the people on my team to know that I expect them to be successful at whatever task I've asked them to accomplish. Don't get me wrong, I understand that there are times when they will fail, and I hope that through failure they will learn better how to succeed. In my book, success means getting the job done and getting results that are expected.

On one leadership website, I saw this quote, "A champion is defined not by their wins but by how they can recover when they fall." The quote was not attributed to anybody, and I honestly don't care who came up with it. It's not a quote I want to live by, and I certainly don't want my people to live by it either. By definition, the number of wins somebody has, as compared to others, is *exactly* how we define a champion.

"Winning is not a sometime thing; it's an all-the-time thing. You don't win once in a while; you don't do things right once in a while; you do them right all the time. Winning is a habit."
-Vince Lombardi

When my children were younger, they played on a soccer team when I was stationed at Fort Irwin in California. The organizers of the league told parents they were not going to keep score during the games. When I asked why, the organizers said because it wasn't important who wins. I immediately told my children, in front of those in charge of the league, that it absolutely matters who wins and that we will be keeping score on our own even if the league did not. You won't be surprised to learn that at the end of the season, everyone received a trophy. What kind of lesson does that teach children? That it's not important to win? It *is* important to win. It's important to try to be the best at whatever you do. Let's get back to keeping score and expecting our organizations to win because winning is important.

Luckily, for America, some of our leaders and politicians today understand the importance of winning and being the best at what they do. Those people are trying to make it clear to everybody that winning is important. Still, there are far too many people who have not figured out that failure, although it occurs on occasion, is not and should not be an acceptable standard. Good leaders demand results from their people and always emphasize the importance of working hard to be number one in whatever they're doing.

Another thing I've heard leadership coaches say is, "Stop judging yourself against others." In fantasyland that might be okay. In the real world, however, your boss is going to judge you by how your performance stacks up against others who are doing the same job. In the real world, good leaders want people on their teams who are the best at what they do. In the real world, how you stack up against other people is how promotions, pay raises and leadership positions are awarded. Being the best at what you do is always a worthy goal.

I played baseball as a youth and throughout high school and college. I was a shortstop and a pitcher. My father came to every game he could come to while I was growing up. He watched me play hundreds of games. Not to brag, but I was a pretty good baseball player. After each game, I would hear other fathers tell their sons that they played good games, even if they didn't. Out of all the games my father watched me play, only once did he tell me I played a great game. In order to gain that praise, I pitched a one-hitter, went 4-for-4 at the plate and hit a home run.

After most games, instead of praising me, he would identify something I needed to work on. But he didn't stop there. After pointing out something he thought I could improve, he would take me out in the backyard when we got home and he'd help me work on those things. He'd hit balls to my right or to my left or make me throw from an unconventional position. He was critical but in a positive way. He wanted me to understand that no matter how good I was, I could always get better. My dad was hard on me, but he wanted me to strive to be the best I could be. Looking back, I'm grateful to him for helping me become the person I am today. He helped me understand the importance of always striving to be my best no matter what I was doing.

"Never let success get to your head. Never let failure get to your heart."
-Tim Tebow

Good leaders understand that how they handle success is just as important as how they handle failure. They understand that they have never arrived. They are always looking to evolve, adapt and improve. Coach Roger Hughes once told me, "Success makes you slow to learn and quick to forget."

When a person experiences success, it can be tempting to grow content and resist change, even though there may be better ways to do things. In the military we called it 'fighting the last war' when people rested on their laurels instead of looking for ways to improve and adapt to conditions that had changed. Even when achieving successes in an organization, a good leader will constantly be looking for ways to improve.

"There are no secrets to success. It is the result of preparation, hard work, and learning from failure."
-Colin Powell

I would suggest that after every major event in your organization you bring the team together to figure out what went well, what went wrong and how to improve the team's performance in the future. In the Army we call this an After Action Review (AAR), but you can call it whatever you want. If you are not currently doing this, you are missing out on opportunities to improve your organization's performance. AARs work, and I would encourage you to implement this kind of discussion after each major event in your organization.

If you don't care about winning, if you don't want to be the best at what you do, then I don't want you on my team. I want to win! I want people on my team who want to win. I don't want to win sometimes; I want to win every time, at everything I do. The leaders for whom I have the greatest respect, whether from the annals of history or those I know personally, have the same attitude. It's simple. Great leaders get results. Period.

Some people I knew used to get angry with me when I would play games with our kids. I didn't care if it was Candy Land, Trouble, Go Fish or Old Maid, I wanted to win. I would tell them that when they beat me, they could say they beat me fair and square because I would never just let them win. My wife agreed to this approach as long as there was no excessive celebrations after a big win.

"Be a yardstick of quality. Some people aren't used to an environment where excellence is expected."
-Steve Jobs

Throughout my career, both in the military and outside the military, my bosses gave me positions of leadership or responsibility because I had a proven record of getting results. If my boss needed something fixed or needed to improve the performance of an organization, he knew I would get the job done. Thanks to my father, I have always understood the importance of being the best I could be at my job as well as how important it is to get results.

When I was a second lieutenant, my platoon had the reputation for being one of the best in the battalion if not the entire brigade. We scored the highest at gunnery, we had the most Expert Infantryman Badge (EIB) winners and during field problems, we were always successful. Unfortunately, we had a platoon in our company that was considered one of the worst in the battalion if not the entire brigade. One day I told my boss that there was absolutely nothing wrong with that platoon except it lacked good leadership. I told him, "If you put me in charge of that platoon, I will show you that it's as good as any in the brigade." He did what I suggested and placed me in charge of that platoon. In three months I had turned that platoon around. As Napoleon said, "There are no bad regiments; there are only bad colonels."

In the end, people will judge your leadership abilities by the results you get. In the real world, results matter. In the real world, not everyone gets a trophy and not everyone is a winner. In the real world, winning matters. Good leaders will always be judged by the results they achieve.

Key Take-aways

- Good leaders will teach and train their people and then motivate them to get results.

- Good leaders will not let failures beat them twice. They don't dwell on failures but learn from them, fix them and move on.

- It's important to cultivate a winning spirit in each of your team members.

- Good leaders strive for perfection even it may not be attainable.

Reflections

- Make sure that the people in your organization understand that, although failures do occur occasionally, it's important to get positive results.

- Take some time to develop a system that helps your team track their progress on their way to success.

- How do you handle failure? How do you handle success? In both cases you should de-brief, find out what occurred and look to get better – even if you were successful.

Commissioning Second Lieutenant Malina Morales – 2019

Notes

Chapter 9

A Leader Never Stops Learning

"Read and re-read the campaigns of Alexander, Hannibal, Caesar, Gustavus Adolphus, Turenne and Frederick. Make them your models. This is the only way to become a great captain and to master the secrets of the art of war."
-Napoleon Bonaparte

GOOD LEADERS NEVER stop learning. They recognize the importance of learning new things and developing new skills. One of the easiest ways to do this is by reading about leadership. I tell people all the time how important it is to read whatever they can get their hands on, whether it's books, magazine articles, bulletins, etc. As the American journalist Margaret Fuller said, "Today a reader, tomorrow a leader." If you find something written about improving your leadership skills, read it. Some may be worthless, but some will be priceless. Take whatever applies to you and put it into practice. Discard what doesn't. In some cases, you can learn plenty from things with which you disagree.

President Harry S. Truman once said, "Not all readers are leaders, but all leaders are readers." All the leaders I know have large libraries — libraries about their professions, about history, about leadership. As Zig Ziglar once said, "Leaders have big libraries; the rest have big screen TVs."

"Disciplining yourself to do what you know is right and important, although difficult, is the high road to pride, self-esteem and personal satisfaction."
-Margaret Thatcher

Never stop reading and learning. Whenever I speak, I encourage people to keep a journal about the books they read. I've done this ever since my years in college. Over the years, not only have I kept a journal of the books I've read, I've taken endless notes and written many comments about the things I've learned from each of those books.

The quote I used at the beginning of this chapter pertains to military leadership. However, there are books, articles and bulletins written about leadership in every profession. It doesn't matter if you want to be a doctor, a businessman, an athlete or follow any other profession. Someone has written something about leadership in that profession. Read as many things as you can get your hands on. I specifically recommend reading autobiographies written by great leaders. These books not only highlight what those leaders accomplished, they explain the hows and the whys behind each story.

I've read hundreds of autobiographies. Many of them feature great military leaders like Patton, MacArthur, Eisenhower, Powell, Schwarzkopf, Grant, Rommel and Guderian. However, I would encourage you to read about leaders who come from outside your profession. In fact, one of my favorite books of all time is the autobiography by Lee Iacocca, the great CEO who revived Chrysler during the 1980s. A lot of people that I speak to don't even know who he was. He was responsible for bringing the Chrysler Motor Company out of bankruptcy in the late 70s and early 80s. As a young man, he worked for Ford as an engineer designing cars. In his autobiography, he tells the story about a car he designed that he wanted Ford to produce. His bosses were not convinced it would sell. He explains how he went about convincing them that his car was a great idea. Can you guess what car he designed? It was the Ford Mustang, one of their best-selling vehicles of all time. To be fair, he did also design the Ford Pinto, of the exploding gas tank variety, but that's another story. Nobody's perfect.

Learning from Experience

When I speak to groups, one of the best pieces of advice I give to men and women is to never avoid a leadership position or opportunity. When I taught Army ROTC cadets, I would occasionally have a project that needed a leader and I would ask for a volunteer. It seems like the same people always raised their hands. It always struck me as odd that everybody didn't immediately raise their hands. After all, they were in the ROTC program to become leaders. If they didn't want to lead, they should have joined some other organization on campus.

"Become the best version of yourself."
-Matthew Kelly

I've always tried to explain to young men and women who aspire to be leaders that great leaders want to lead. They don't want to lead sometimes; they want to lead all the time. It's what leaders do! It's how they think and how they operate. They lead. All the time. I've always wanted to lead, no matter the situation. Now, trust me, I know when I go home every night and walk through my front door, I'm not the leader anymore. I know who the leader in my house is and it's not me. There's a reason I've been happily married for so many years. However, in the morning, when I leave the house and head off to work, I want to be in charge again and be the best leader I can be.

Good leaders understand that practice makes perfect. If you want to be the best baseball player or musician or teacher, then you must practice. That is how anybody becomes the best at something. It's no different with leadership. You can read about leadership; you can learn leadership principles in a classroom; you can observe other leaders in action. All of these things are important, but the only way to truly develop great leadership skills is by leading. Leaders will want to lead all the time. Good leaders will figure out through practice what works and what doesn't. While reading and learning about leadership is important, practicing leadership is the best way to become a good leader.

"Leaders never stop learning."
-Christine Caine

Many times throughout my career, I've had the opportunity to watch successful leaders make decisions or do things that I thought were outstanding. During those times, I would make mental notes so that in the future, when I was in a position of leadership, I could make similar sound decisions. Far too often, I've witnessed leaders make foolish decisions or do things horribly wrong. In those cases, I also made mental notes so I could avoid making those mistakes in the future. Good leaders will catalog good and bad learning experiences and draw from them when in positions of leadership.

Figuring Out What Works for You

Just as there are many definitions of leadership, there are many leadership styles as well. A big part of being a successful leader is figuring out your personal leadership style. When it comes to leadership styles, there is no one-size-fits-all formula and no absolute guarantees for success. The leadership style that works for me may not work for you. The leadership style that works for you may not work for me. Your leadership style will be your own, adjusted for the differences in organizations and personnel with whom you work.

Keeping a Leadership Journal

Good leaders document their successes and failures. I started a leadership journal during my years as a cadet. I would encourage anybody who aspires to lead to keep some sort of leadership journal. Whether you're a young man or woman just starting out in your career or if you've been in leadership positions for years, a leadership journal can be a valuable tool.

Every time I've had the opportunity to listen to an important leader speak, I would take notes and then transcribe them into my journal. I've had the opportunity to listen to some great leaders over the years, both military and civilian, and continue the practice to this today. You're never too old to learn more about leadership or use something someone else has done to improve your leadership skills. I also enjoy keeping quotes about leadership in my journal. Several times over the years, when I've taken a leadership role in a new organization, I will pull out my journal and look up things that can help me in my new role.

"Leadership and learning are indispensable to each other."
-John F. Kennedy

Being a successful leader is all about learning and developing the skills required to lead. There are no shortcuts to success as it relates to leadership. Learning the necessary skills won't always come easy. If there were shortcuts and if it was easy, anybody could become a great leader. Never turn down the chance to learn new skills and continue to develop the skills you already have. The people you lead deserve to have the best leader possible.

Key Take-aways

- Good leaders are always looking to build upon and improve their leadership skills.

- Good leaders always want to lead.

- Good leaders never stop learning.

- Consume leadership literature whenever you can.

Reflections

- When presented the opportunity to be in a position of leadership, never turn it down.

- Look for ways to continue building and developing your leadership skills.

- What is the last piece of leadership literature you read? Find your next leadership book and commit some time each day to reading it.

With Kelly, my Napoleon's Corporal
Christmas - 2019

Notes

Chapter 10

Concluding Thoughts

"Men make history and not the other way around. In periods where there is no leadership, society stands still. Progress occurs when courageous, skillful leaders seize the opportunity to change things for the better."
-Harry S Truman

WHEN I SPEAK to groups, especially groups of young people, I tell them that leaders are not born, they're made. I make sure they understand that every great leader started exactly where they are. Becoming a leader is not a destination, it's a journey.

Becoming a good leader does not just happen overnight; it's a never-ending process. Becoming a good leader is all about learning leadership principles and skills, practicing those skills and then learning from those experiences to build new skills, all while developing a personal leadership style.

"The expert in anything was once a beginner."
-Helen Hayes

I will go back to a quote I introduced earlier, the one that inspired my leadership lecture and this book, "Great leadership handed down from generation to generation is what develops great nations."

This quote has always inspired me. Developing future leaders has long been my passion. This quote pertains to other young men and women as well – those who aspire to lead and then teach the next generation to lead.

At some point, the current generation of leaders is going to hand the reigns of leadership to the next generation. If you are an aspiring leader, it's up to you to prepare yourself in order to be ready to meet that challenge. You owe it to yourself and to those you will lead.

Ralph Nader once said, "The function of leadership is to produce more leaders, not more followers." I can think of no greater responsibility than that. Take it seriously and teach the next generation well. The future depends on it.

Leadership is About Selfless Service

General Bruce C. Clarke put it best when he said, "Rank is given to you to enable you to better serve those above and below you. It is not given for you to practice your idiosyncrasies." You can substitute 'leadership position' for 'rank,' if you like, but the concept remains the same.

"The leader sees leadership as responsibility rather than as rank and privilege."
-Peter Drucker

To repeat an earlier sentiment, leadership is all about selfless service. Good leaders will do more than just give lip-service to this concept. They will live it. It's a vital part of leadership that can't be overstated.

Making a Difference

I've been involved with developing future leaders of the Army through the ROTC program for 13 years now. I've had the honor of commissioning hundreds of second lieutenants during that time. One of the last things I tell new officers is, "Go out there and make a difference." By definition, leaders are change-makers. I tell them to make a difference in the lives of their people, make a difference in their organizations and make a difference in this great country of ours. Great leaders want to make things better for the people that work for them and for the organizations they serve. Great leaders make a difference.

"Great leadership usually starts with a willing heart, a positive attitude, and a desire to a make a difference."
-Mac Anderson

One Final Thought

What kind of leader do you want to be? Do you want to be the leader who always does the right thing, even when the right thing may not be in your personal best interest? Do you want to be the leader that sets good examples in everything you do every day? Do you want to be the leader who holds the people in your organization to high standards?

What kind of leader do you want to be? The answer is up to you. You are the one who must decide which type of leader you want to be. You can be the leader who is just there for a paycheck or the extra privileges. Or you can be the leader who is there for a higher purpose. The leader who honestly cares about right and wrong. The leader who actually cares about the welfare of the organization and its people. The leader who truly wants to make a difference in the lives of others. The leader who will take responsibility for teaching and training the next generation of leaders. To that end, the decision is yours. It's my sincere hope that you choose to lead.

Success is never owned; it is rented and the rent is due every day."
-Rory Vaden

It's my sincere hope that you become the leader you were meant to be, for the sake of the organizations and people you lead and for the sake of the next generation of leaders that will follow in your footsteps. The future of our country depends on it.

Key Take-aways

- Becoming a good leader is a journey, not a destination.

- Good leaders look for ways to make a difference.

- The kind of leader you become will have second and third-order effects on the people you lead, the organization you work for and possibly your country.

Reflections

- Define what kind of leader you want to be, write it down

and refer back to it often to help you stay focused on what defines you as a leader.

- Look for ways to improve as a leader a little bit each day.
- Make the decision to be the best leader you can be, and commit to that decision every day.

Fishing the mangroves of Daytona Beach, FL - 2020

Keepers!

Notes

Quotes Resources

John Quincey Adams (July 11, 1767 – February 23, 1848) was an American statesman and diplomat who served as the sixth President of the United States from 1825 – 1829. (p. v)

Mac Anderson (October 8, 1919 – December 21, 1979) was a New Zealand cricketer. (p. 153)

Joel A. Baker is an American futurist, author and filmmaker. (p. 29)

Perry Belcher is an investor and marketing specialist who is also the co-founder of Digital Marketer. (p. 114)

Warren Bennis (March 8, 1925 – July 31, 2014) was an American scholar, organizational consultant and author, widely regarded as a pioneer in the contemporary field of Leadership Studies. (pp. 1, 2)

Napoleon Bonaparte (August 15, 1769 – May 5, 1821) was a French statesman and military leader. Considered one of the greatest military leaders in the history of the world, he was the Emperor of France from 1804-1814 and again briefly during 1815. (pp. 88, 136, 140).

Omar N. Bradley (February 12, 1893 – April 8, 1981) graduated from the United States Military Academy at West Point in 1915 and was a senior officer in the United States Army during World War II. He rose to the rank of General of the Army (five-star general) and was the first Chairman of the Joint Chiefs of Staff. (pp. 25, 46)

Richard Branson is an English business magnate, investor, author and philanthropist. (p. 73)

Christine Caine is an Australian activist, evangelist, author and international speaker. (p. 144)

Andrew Carnegie (November 25, 1835 – August 11, 1919) was a Scottish-American industrialist and philanthropist who led the expansion of the American steel industry in the 19th century. (p. 74)

Winston Churchill (November 30, 1874 – January 24, 1965) was a British statesman, Army officer, and writer. He was Prime Minister of the United Kingdom from 1940-1945, during World War II. (p. 129)

Bruce C. Clarke (April 29, 1901 – March 17, 1988) was a United States Army four-star general who served in World War I, World War II and the Korean War. (p. 152)

Stephen Covey (October 24, 1932 – July 16, 2012) was an American educator, author, businessman and speaker. (p. 61)

Bantz J. Craddock is a retired United States Army four-star general who served in Desert Shield/Desert Storm and in Kosovo. (pp. 60, 83, 121)

Peter Drucker (November 19, 1909 – November 11, 2005) was an Austrian management consultant, educator and author. (p. 152)

John Eades is a contemporary American author and speaker. (p. 65)

Dwight D. Eisenhower (October 14, 1890 – March 28, 1969) was a United States Army five-star general who was the Supreme Allied Commander for the D-Day invasion during World War II. He eventually served as the 34th President of the United States. (p. 2)

Ralph Waldo Emerson (May 25, 1803 – April 27, 1882) was an American essayist, lecturer, philosopher and poet who led the transcendentalist movement in the mid-19th century. (p. 32)

Hans Finzel is an author, speaker, podcaster and trusted authority in the field of leadership. He recently completed 20 years as president and CEO of the nonprofit World Venture. (p. 121)

Margaret Fuller (May 23, 1810 – July 19, 1850) was an American journalist and women's rights advocate. (p. 141)

Christopher "Chris" Fussel is a former SEAL officer in the United States Navy who served as the aide-de-camp for then Lieutenant General Stanley McChrystal. (p. 68)

John W. Gardner (October 8, 1912 – February 16, 2002) served as an officer in the United States Marine Corps during World War II and was Secretary of Health, Education and Welfare (HEW) under President Lyndon Johnson. (p. 2)

Bill Gates is an American business magnate, software developer and philanthropist. He's best known as the chairman, CEO and co-founder of Microsoft Corporation. (p. 88)

Arnold Glasgow (1905 - 1998) was an American businessman and author. (p. 96)

Helen Hayes (October 10, 1900 – March 17, 1993) was an American actress whose career spanned 80 years. She was one of only 16 people who have won an Emmy, a Grammy, an Oscar, and a Tony Award. (p. 151)

Heraclitus of Ephesus (535-475 B.C.) was an ancient Greek, pre-Socratic, Ionian philosopher. (p. 37)

Theodore Hesburgh (May 25, 1917 – February 26, 2015) was an ordained Catholic priest best known for his service as the president of the University of Notre Dame from 1952-1987. (p. 26)

Gordon B. Hinckley (June 23, 1910 – January 27, 2008) was an American religious leader and author who served as the 15th President of The Church of Jesus Christ of Latter-day Saints. (p. 13)

Roger Hughes is an American college football coach and former player. He is currently the head football coach for Stetson University. (p. 133)

Phil Jackson is a former NBA player, coach and executive. As the head coach for the Chicago Bulls, he led them to six championship titles. (p. 111)

Steve Jobs (February 24, 1955 – October 5, 2011) was an American business magnate, industrial designer, investor and media proprietor. He was chairman, CEO and co-founder of Apple, Inc. (p. 135)

Michael Jordan is an American businessman and former professional basketball player. He played 15 seasons in the NBA, winning six championships with the Chicago Bulls. (p. 19)

Matthew Kelly is an Australian author, motivational speaker and business consultant. (p. 143)

John F. Kennedy (May 29, 1917 – November 22, 1963) was an American politician who served as a naval officer during World War II and served as the 35th President of the United States. (pp. 37, 146)

Ray Krock (October 5, 1902 – January14, 1984) was an American businessman. He is best known for his leadership in the McDonald's Corporation. (p. 21)

Abraham Lincoln (February 12, 1809 – April 15, 1865) was an American statesman and lawyer who served as the 16th President of the United States. (p. 51)

Vince Lombardi (June 11, 1913 – September 3, 1970) was an American football coach and executive in the National Football League. He is best known as the head coach of the Green Bay Packers during the 1960s where he led the team to three straight NFL Championships, including winning the first two Super Bowls. (pp. 110, 130, 131)

Douglas MacArthur (January 26, 1880 – April 5, 1964) was a five-star general in the United States Army. He was Chief of Staff of the Army during the 1930s and played a prominent role in the Pacific theater during World War II. He was also served as the Superintendent of the United States Military Academy at West Point from 1919-1922 and was the Commander-in-Chief of the United Nations Command during the Korean War from 1950-1951. (p. 3)

George C. Marshall (December 31, 1880 – October 16, 1959) was an American soldier and statesman. He graduated from Virginia Military Institute and rose to the rank of General of the Army (five-star general) and was Chief of Staff of the Army during World War II. After the war, he became the 50th Secretary of State under President Truman. (p. 119)

Joseph Martz is a retired United States Army three-star general who served for 36 years. He is now a successful businessman who started Martz & Associates Consulting. (p. 42)

John C. Maxwell is an American author, motivational speaker and pastor. (pp. 6, 16, 82, 84)

Oakland Vincent McCulloch is a former Army officer and West Point graduate who is now a leader in the business world. (p. 91)

J. P. Morgan (April 17, 1837 – March 31, 1913) was an American financier and banker who dominated corporate finance on Wall Street throughout the Gilded Age. (p. 124)

Christopher Morley (May 5, 1890 – March 28, 1957) was an American journalist, novelist, essayist and poet. (p. 62)

Ralph Nader is an American political activist, author, lecturer, lawyer and former candidate for President of the United States. (p. 151)

Caileigh Nicholson is a graduate from the University of South Alabama who has held several positions in the business world. (p. 116)

George S. Patton, Jr. (November 11, 1885 – December 21, 1945) was a graduate of the United States Military Academy at West Point. He rose to the rank of four-star general in the U.S. Army and served in several key leadership positions during World War II. (p. 35, 80)

Colin Powell is an American politician, diplomat and retired four-star general who served as the 65th United States Secretary of State. (pp. 5, 95, 134)

David Powell is a retired United States Army Master Sergeant who is now a successful businessman. (pp. vii and 151)

Ronald Reagan (February 6. 1911 – June 5, 2004) was an American politician who served as the 40th President of the United States from 1981-1989. (p. 80)

Erwin Rommel (November 15, 1891 – October 14, 1944) was a German general and military theorist rising to the rank of Field Marshall during World War II. (p. 36)

Theodore Roosevelt (October 27, 1858 – January 6, 1919) was an American statesman, conservationist, soldier, historian and writer who served as the 26th President of the United States. (p. 34)

Norman Schwarzkopf (August 22, 1934 – December 27, 2012) was a United States Army four-star general who was the commander of the United States Central Command during Operation Desert Shield/Desert Storm. (p. 1)

George Bernard Shaw (July 26, 1856 – November 2, 1950) was an Irish playwright, critic and political activist. (p. 53)

Simon Sinek is a British-American author and inspirational speaker. (pp. 41, 78, 115)

Socrates (470-399 BC) was a Greek philosopher from Athens who is one of the founders of Western philosophy. (p. 39)

Andy Stanley is the founder and senior pastor of North Point Ministries, a nondenominational evangelical Christian church in the Atlanta area and an author of over 20 books. (p. 59)

Alexis de Tocqueville (July 29, 1805 – April 16, 1859) was a French aristocrat, diplomat, political scientist, political philosopher and historian. He is best known for his two-book series *Democracy in America*. (p. 21)

Tim Tebow is an American professional baseball player, former professional football player and broadcaster who won the Heisman Trophy in 2007. (p. 133)

Margaret Thatcher (October 13, 1925 – April 8, 2014) was a British politician and stateswoman who served as Prime Minister of the United Kingdom from 1979 to 1990. (p. 141)

Brian Tracy is a Canadian-American motivational speaker and self-development author. (pp. 47, 97)

Bill Treasurer is a speaker, author, consultant and CEO of Giant Leap Consulting. (p. 14)

Harry S Truman (May 8, 1884 – December 26, 1972) was the 33rd President of the United States from 1945-1953. (pp. 141, 150)

Lao Tzu (believed to have lived in the 4th century BC) was an ancient Chinese philosopher and writer. (p. 83)

Rory Vaden is a bestselling author, speaker and co-founder of Southwestern Consulting. (p. 154)

George Villiers (August 28, 1592 – August 23, 1628) was the first Duke of Buckingham. He was a courtier, statesman and patron of the arts. He was a favorite of King James I of England. (p. 113)

Sam Walton (March 29, 1918 – April 5, 1992) was an American businessman and entrepreneur best known for founding the retailers Walmart and Sam's Club. (p. 120)

Jack Welch (November 19, 1935 – March 1, 2020) was an American business executive, chemical engineer and writer. He was Chairman and CEO of General Electric (GE) between 1981 and 2001. (p. 12)

Robin Williams (July 21, 1951 – August 11, 2014) was an American comedian and actor. (p. 101)

John "Jocko" Willink is an American author and retired naval officer who served in the Navy SEALs. (p. 84)

John Wooden (October 14, 1910 – June 4, 2010) was an American basketball player and coach. He is best known as the head basketball coach for the UCLA Bruins where he won 10 National Collegiate Athletic Association (NCAA) national championships. (p. 85)

Zig Ziglar (November 6, 1926 – November 28, 2012) was an American author, salesman and motivational speaker. (pp. 117, 141)